T4-AUC-246

Artists,

Craftsmen

and Technocrats

Artists,

Craftsmen

and Technocrats

The Dreams, Realities and Illusions of Leadership

PATRICIA PITCHER

Published in 1995 by
Stoddart Publishing Co. Limited
34 Lesmill Road
Toronto, Canada
M3B 2T6
(416) 445-3333
445-5967 (fax)

Stoddart Books are available for bulk purchase for sales promotions, premiums, fundraising, and seminars. For details, contact the Special Sales Department at the above address.

Canadian Cataloguing in Publication Data

Pitcher, Patricia C.
Artists, craftsmen and technocrats: the dreams, realities and illusions of leadership

ISBN 0-7737-2858-9

1. Leadership.　2. Management.　I. Title
HD57.7.P57 1995　　658.4'092　　C95-930056-2

Cover Design: Bill Douglas/The Bang
Printed and bound in Canada

Stoddart Publishing gratefully acknowledges the support of the Canada Council, the Ontario Ministry of Culture, Tourism, and Recreation, Ontario Arts Council, and Ontario Publishing Centre in the development of writing and publishing in Canada.

Contents

Foreword

I had the pleasure of supervising this work in its original form as a doctoral thesis. So I am perfectly biased. *I know* it is a critically important piece of work, tackled with a sophistication and elegance that is rare in the management literature. If the message of this book can be taken to heart by people in important places, our organizations will become entirely different and, in my opinion, much more effective places.

A leader has to be one of two things. He either has to be a brilliant visionary himself, a truly creative strategist, in which case he can do what he likes and get away with it. Or else she has to be a true empowerer, who can bring out the best in others. Managers who are neither can be deadly in organizations that need energy and change. In this book, Pat calls the first Artists and the second Craftsmen, the third Technocrats. She shows in a pointed, deep study of a large financial institution how the Technocrats killed what the Artists built and the Craftsmen protected.

We have to understand these different management styles and what each can do to organizations. If you care about what's happening to business and other organizations in the western world, this is a book you will want to read and cherish.

HENRY MINTZBERG
McGill University
Montreal

Preface

Not too long ago a journalist said to me, "Didn't you used to be Pat Johnston?" Yes, I said. "You were quite a firebrand in those days." Yes, I said, I was. What a strange mixture of emotions this evoked in me: pride, wonder, sadness, even shame. In the decade 1973 to 1983, I had been a crusader for various causes: first as a "socialist" with Stephen Lewis and the New Democratic Party, then as a "capitalist" at the Toronto Stock Exchange, then as an ardent Canadian "nationalist" with Walter Gordon and the now-defunct Canadian Institute for Economic Policy, and finally as a spokesman for "small business." It was principally in this last guise that I achieved notoriety as a firebrand. Then, at the peak of my so-called glory, solicited on all sides by the siren songs of money and prestige, I dropped out. I got off the merry-go-round. All work, scientific or creative, is consciously or unconsciously autobiographical; this book, and the study on which it is based, is no accident.

John Maynard Keynes once quipped that "practical men, who believe themselves to be quite exempt from any intellectual influences, are usually the slaves of some defunct economist." Prophetic words. Many had become his slaves before we became Milton Friedman's. In fact, in my experience, we are adept at being slaves to all sorts of ideologies. During those years I spent as a crusader I discovered that what is real, obvious, pressing, true, is usually bound and gagged and sacrificed on the altar of some theory or other. I'm reminded of the joke about the economist who, when told of the 1987 stock market crash, replied, "Yes, maybe so, but the real question is, can it happen in theory?!" We were all, myself included (thus the shame), rushing around shouting theories at one another, and the din was excruciating. The screaming was so loud that a practical man like Joe Clark could not be heard. When Clark, then prime minister, talked quietly about Canada being a "community of communities," it was too real, too true. It wasn't "clever" enough. We preferred the seemingly dispassionate, arid intellectualizations and "brilliant" centralist theorizing of Pierre Elliott Trudeau. Why do we worship brilliant over wise? The brilliant ideologues of centralism beget the ideologues of separatism; Trudeau's rigidity is partly responsible for the enduring appeal of Quebec separatism. The ideologues of the public sector produce the ideologues of the free market and vice versa; right-wing excesses created social-democratic and left-wing liberal excesses, which in turn spawned Margaret Thatcher and Ronald Reagan and Brian Mulroney, and now the "left" is mad about it? The ideology of "big business" produces the ideology of "small business" and so on and so on and so on, *ad infinitum*. Common Sense, which has had an undeservedly bad reputation ever since it thought the earth was flat, gets squeezed out of the middle. It was all so useless and dispiriting. I had to get out of the noise. Pat, I said, get thee to a nunnery. So, I went to McGill. This book is the result of my decade away.

PATRICIA PITCHER, PHD
Montreal

Introduction

Still more do I regret the failure to convey the sense of organization, the dramatic and aesthetic feeling that surpasses the possibilities of exposition, which derives from the intimate, habitual interested experience. It is evident that many lack an interest in the science of organizing, not perceiving the significant elements. They miss the structure of the symphony, the art of its composition, and the skill of its execution, because they cannot hear the tones.

CHESTER BARNARD, *THE FUNCTIONS OF THE EXECUTIVE*

This book, and the study on which it is based, is the product, as are all such works, of a personal odyssey. I had decided to do a doctorate in management and, like most practitioners, really hadn't the faintest idea what the academics said about managing. Being exposed to it for the first time in 1986 was a shock. It sure missed the "tone" of organization. With rare but welcome exceptions, there were no real *people* in most of the management literature. There were recipes. There were theories galore. Systems. Functions. Roles. There was no passion, no joy, no triumph, no envy, no lust, no hate, no greed and avarice, cowardice or dreams. Like the little old lady in the Wendy's commercial, I cried, "Where's the beef?" This stuff did not in any way conform to what I had seen and lived "out there." It seemed to reduce leadership to a task anyone could be taught and management to a kind of paint-by-numbers art — stay within the lines (of reengineering or of participative management, for example) and you will have a pretty

1

picture. Tell that to Picasso and Van Gogh, I thought. Tell that to Proust or Dostoevsky. Tell it to René Lévesque, Abraham Lincoln, Winston Churchill and Charles de Gaulle. By extension, tell it to Lee Iacocca, Stephen Jobs, Carlo de Benedetti and Jean-Marie Poitras. It won't wash. It's not true. Paint-by-numbers became my guiding metaphor as I began a long search for the golden fleece of real art and real artists in management.

Of course, when you take a trip, you see things along the way. The study of art helped me to see the real artists all right, but it also gave me an intellectual lens through which I saw their fellow travellers, the Craftsmen. That discovery would prove critical, as you will see later. In addition, the lens helped me to see the paint-by-numbers managers — the enemies of both art and craft — the Technocrats, those for whom "the technical side of an issue takes precedence over the social and human consequences."[1] I use that word "enemies" deliberately. A lot of people lament the absence of great leaders today. Many of us cast a nostalgic eye on the Churchills, the de Gaulles, the Lincolns, the John A. Macdonalds. Great leaders have always been, and always will be, rare — the cream that rose to the top before milk and men were homogenized. But, as I hope to show here, they are more numerous than it first appears, and cream is not the only substance that has a tendency to rise to the surface. Leaders have powerful enemies. There's a war going on out there and it is not for the faint of heart. The good guys do not always win.

It's exceedingly important to understand this war. Ever since the "discipline" of management muscled its way into universities, much to the consternation of many scholars past and present — Thorstein Veblen for one, Allan Bloom for another — it has gained more and more respectability. If management is a "science," then it stands to reason that everywhere there is a need for management there is a need for the science. So much has this become the prevailing view that a recent French prime minister could say with a straight face, "*On ne gère jamais assez*" — we can never manage too much.[2] In North America at least (for reasons that we will explore later, I think Europe and Japan are partly inoculated), we have brought the science of management to government and to social institutions like hospitals and schools. Now, it's true that some disciplines within management do have more of the character of a formal science — finance, accounting, even marketing — but general management is not one of them. To take what we have allegedly proved in general management and graft it onto the public life is to commit a cardinal sin. To imagine, as some do, that modern management techniques eliminate the need for inspiration, intuition, judgement and the careful selection of the best people is not just dangerous for corporations, national competitiveness and economic prosperity, it is very dangerous for our societies as a whole. We need to recover some truth.

Of course there are all kinds of truths — literary truth, spiritual and religious truth, scientific truth, sociological truth — and no one can pretend to capture Truth with a capital "T." The truth I describe in this book is a small truth, a partial truth. I describe and analyse a cast of characters who interact on an organizational stage and I describe their interactions as the working out of different character types: the Artist, the Craftsman and the Technocrat. You will notice points of interpenetration of the philosophical and the historical. Of course, I believe that philosophy and history write on the mind of modern man, but I also believe that man has his own pen and writes his own story too. If not, how could those who criticize our era do so? If we are all nothing but the product of our age, how could they see it? Is it simply that they are smarter than the rest of us? I don't think so. They bring their own characters to bear upon a reading of history. They see what, in some sense, they want to see. They feel what others do not feel, and they therefore think what others do not think. Man is neither a Lockean *tabula rasa* nor a sociologist's *tabula rasa*. He brings something of his own to the game. He brings his character.

I found out early on that "management" had seemed to wish to do away with character. It seemed to wish to carve man up into his various pieces: the eyes that see, the hand that executes, the head that thinks (conveniently forgetting the heart that feels). Having done so, management went on to develop recipes to address the parts: teach people how to see better, teach them how to think better, teach them how to behave and to feel, and to be nice. Even teach them how to have vision. Well, the hand, the head and the heart come in packages, and the package is called character. It's unrealistic to think that you can teach a stone-hearted man to be nice and to have vision. At least, not in this lifetime and certainly not in a management-training course. If, today, we want managers who are open-minded, we have to select those who are; this was once self-evident.

Part I, The Players and the Plot, is descriptive. In Chapter One we find the Artist, the "administrative genius." He's imaginative, intuitive, funny, inspiring, exciting and emotionally volatile. He's visionary. He can be moody, sometimes solitary. Men as seemingly diverse as Abraham Lincoln and René Lévesque give some idea of what my Artist might look like. Some have said that Lévesque was too emotional, that his ideas lacked clarity and order.[3] Most of the Artists you will meet in these pages would be dismissed and discounted and run out of town on the same grounds.

Chapter Two describes the organizational Craftsman: dedicated, trustworthy, honest, stable, realistic and wise. We will see that these qualities are very much in disrepute, in part because modernity cannot suffer authority, discipline, tradition — the craft virtues.

Chapter Three portrays the Technocrat. Cerebral, stiff, uncompromising, intense, determined, hardheaded, meticulous, often brilliant, he pretends he wants "reason" to dominate "emotion," but this is a lie. All sane people want reason to be in the driver's seat; the Technocrat wants, passionately, for reason to *crush* passion.

The next chapter puts all three characters into perspective, in relation to one another. It shows what they think of one another and foreshadows the kinds of conflicts that will emerge.

Part II, The Play, begins by describing how these three character types worked together and against one another over the fifteen-year life of a multibillion-dollar, multinational organization. It shows how the technocratic mentality ultimately drives out everything else. It shows, as well, how the Craftsman gets caught in the crossfire between Artists and Technocrats.

In Chapter Six I try to explain the reasons for the technocratic victory and spell out its organizational consequences. I argue that the Technocrat manages to high-jack the organization with our support and complicity, and that the pseudoscience of futurism must now bear part of the blame.

Part III, The Moral of the Story, spells out some of the consequences for the rest of us. The first chapter revisits current theories of leadership and argues that they have become the cure that is worse than the disease, while the next chapter reexamines some popular buzzwords like "participative management" and tries to show that all-purpose management recipes are counterproductive. It demonstrates that management is difficult, multiple, particular — a craft, and neither a science nor an art — and still demands the wise selection of the right people for the job.

Having shown in Chapter Ten that selection, not training, is the centrepiece of good management, I then outline in Chapter Eleven what is left for education — how nurture can shape nature.

Part IV shifts gears. Chapter Twelve, An Ode to Craftsmanship, argues against miracles and oracles and argues for a restoration of reality-testing, followed by a few reflections on the social and economic implications of craftsmanship. The final chapter, on "cocooning," is a private word to baby boomers.

My Conclusion is brief, because I don't have any magic potions to offer. So, what you will *not* find here are any new formulae for managing: no appeals to "flat structures," no "reengineering," no "participative management," no instant just-add-water leadership recipes. You will find description and analysis. Management scholars have been too hasty in their prescriptions; it's all very well and good to tell managers what they should be doing, but what if the people out there are simply incapable of following the recipe? This book is deliberately and consciously descriptive because description is the best ally of healthy change. Accurate, compelling description can change the world. Accurate description can help people to better understand their world, recognizing that it is they, not us, who are best placed to judge what to do with it.

I've used more imagery and metaphors than technical language, because technical language, though it seems impressive, often does little to enlighten. Pseudoscientific language is not more "objective" than poetic language, and "we delude ourselves if we think that philosophical or critical language for these matters is somehow more hard-edged and more free from personal index than that of poets or novelists."[4] Further, the tone of this book is passionate. I believe that passion, caring about something, *increases* our ability to see clearly. If we care, we look more *care*fully. We are more, not less, "scientific." This, too, is now a sacrilege.

Now I'm going to expose you to a short intellectual travelogue that describes the conceptual and methodological underpinnings of my research. Those who dislike guided tours can skip to Chapter One.

WHY ART?

In *The Courage to Be*, theologian Paul Tillich wrote:

> They [Kierkegaard, Nietzsche, Bergson] realized that a process was going on in which people were transformed into things, into pieces of reality which pure science can calculate and technical science can control. The idealistic wing of bourgeois thinking made of the person a vessel in which universals find a more or less adequate place. The naturalistic wing of bourgeois thinking made of the person an empty field into which sense impressions enter and prevail according to the degree of their intensity. In both cases the individual self is an empty space and the bearer of something which is not himself. . . . Idealism and naturalism are alike in their attitude to the existing person; both of them eliminate his infinite significance and make him a space through which something else passes.

I sensed that what Tillich said applied to management, as well, but outmanned and outgunned, in the beginning of my research I could do nothing but beat a strategic retreat. The first rule of combat is "Know thine enemy." Well, that takes time. Fortunately I had it. I set out to discover from whence came management's exceedingly limited vision of man. Of course, that meant reading "the greats." In management, they are Fayol, Taylor, Barnard and Selznik; going forward in time, they are "the moderns," Harvard's Ken Andrews and Michael Porter, McGill's Henry Mintzberg and USC's Warren Bennis. Peter Drucker and Herbert Simon straddle the two eras.

I got stuck at Herbert Simon. Little known in the outside world, Simon is a giant in management. You can feel his influence everywhere. "Bounded rationality" is his flag, and his flagship led a whole fleet of cognitive psychologists into management's quiet harbour. In 1960 he told us in his book *The New Science of Management Decision* that unlike the management of yore, modern management would rely on training more than on selection, on information systems more than on intuition, on planning more than on judgement.[5] Here is an abridged version of a little table of his:

Types of Decisions	Decision-making Techniques	
	Traditional	Modern
Nonprogrammed:	1) Judgement, intuition and creativity	Heuristic problem-solving techniques applied to;
One-shot, ill-structured novel, policy decisions	2) Rules of thumb	a) training human decision makers
Handled by general problem-solving processes	3) Selection and training of executives	b) constructing heuristic computer programs

Notice the pejorative phrasing, juxtaposing "traditional" (bad) against "modern" (good); "heuristic computer programs" are modern, judgement and intuition, old-fashioned. Spiritual descendant of Frederick Winslow Taylor, Simon took Taylor's principles of "scientific management" from the shop floor to the senior reaches of the organization. Michael Porter was later to take them right into the boardroom with his scientific management of strategy and the "one best way." More on that later.

For the moment, I was stalled. I approached Simon with kid gloves. For as a child of the radical sixties and early seventies, I had learned a hard lesson. Those of us infatuated with Marx had adopted first Keynes and then John Kenneth Galbraith as our economic gurus. Milton Friedman was our diabolical archenemy. Then, one day in the late seventies, I went to listen to Friedman. This man was also a giant. The breadth and depth of his scholarship, the power of his analysis, were breathtaking. He made his left-wing critics and questioners in the audience look like intellectual pygmies. It was a very sobering experience. I realized Simon was a Goliath and I had no intention of tackling him with a slingshot. I wasn't sure that God was on my side.

All I knew was that Simon was wrong. Wrong about what? Everything. Wrong how? I don't know. You know how you can have a nagging, uncomfortable feeling about something but it's impossible to explain or define? Like the fairy tale where the "true" princess could only be discovered by putting a pea under a stack of mattresses and finding out whether or not she could sleep. Well, without comparing myself to a true princess, I couldn't sleep. So I went looking for causes. I started my search in Simon's bibliography: tell me who a man reads and I'll tell you what he thinks. Herbert Simon's mentors were, and are, cognitive psychologists. Maybe by reading cognitive psychology, I would discover the nature of the pea.

I turned for guidance to H. Gardner's *The Mind's New Science*,[6] the somewhat pretentious title of a survey of cognitive science's accomplishments, and basically discovered that here man was, more or less and usually less, an adequate "information processor." He was a brain, a mind-machine without a heart, a Lockean "empty field into which sense impressions enter and prevail according to the degree of their intensity and. . . ." So, if man is a mind-machine, it stands to reason that the machine can be "fixed" or perfected, and therefore, training becomes a credible substitute for selection. Perfectly logical, you say. Well, yes, if the premise were true. But it isn't. Man is not like a machine; he has a heart and emotions, and that heart influences what he sees and thinks. Cognitive psychology is an assembly kit that comes batteries not included: no morality, no emotion, no will to make the machine run. It freely admits that it had to set aside "the influence of affective factors or emotions, the contribution of historical and cultural factors, and the role of background context in which particular actions and thoughts occur."[7] Okay, so to proceed with any research we have to make some simplifying assumptions, but come on, affect, history, volition, judgement, context, culture, history? What's left worth knowing?

In any event, all this stuff had been imported directly and unadulterated into management research. Man as information processor is the subtle and sometimes not-so-subtle intellectual underpinning. Thus in strategy, for example, you don't need judgement or intuition if you have adequate information and you process it adequately. This notion is best exemplified by Michael Porter's enormously successful books *Competitive Advantage* and *Competitive Strategy*.[8] Here we find an exhaustive, and exhausting, recipe for collecting all the information managers should accumulate in order to deduce a strategy. If the right information is collected and the analysis is done right, anyone can sit in the executive suite no matter what his character or temperament. It's a useful recipe for novices, for students, and a wonderful and useful pedagogical device for professors of management. It's also a great tool for management consultants hired to develop a strategy for an organization operating in a sector of which they have no firsthand knowledge. And it's essential for peripatetic managers, who flit from

9

one sector to another, for it gives them a way to acquire some superficial understanding of each new sector. But I have never met a seasoned manager who needed it, used it or valued it. This became another clue as to what may be going on in the "science" of management.

Anyway, *The Mind's New Science* turned out to be a dud, and I'd taken a year-long detour down a blind alley. Nothing left but to retrace my steps and take Frost's road "less traveled by." If cognitive psychology was an assembly kit that came batteries not included (emotion and volition), I needed to find out more about affect, or feeling, and the role that it plays in human mentation, judgement, decision-making. Some evidence emerged from experimental psychology.[9] One researcher has shown that emotion affects all kinds of judgements, decision-making, strategy and willingness to take risk:

> In combination with other data showing effects of positive affect on word-association, memory and creative problem-solving, these data support our hypothesis that positive affect is associated with cognitive reorganization such that more relations among concepts or ideas are seen than is the case under neutral-affect conditions.[10]

Here, we're a long way from the information-processing model. And yet, isn't managing all about "creative problem-solving"? Isn't "cognitive reorganization" exactly what we need faced with the manifest failure of old solutions to competitive, and social, challenges? What literature could I explore that addresses this dicey, delicate, intricate relation between feeling and thought?

If modern cognitive psychology has largely conceived of man as machine, depth psychology, or dynamic psychology, has been from the beginning more interested in the ghost that inhabits the machine. And from the beginning, it was interested in emotion, affect, the batteries, what makes the system move. A psychopath who murders little children does not lack information — he knows he is breaking the law and all of our moral codes — he lacks conscience. Someone suffering from paranoid delusions is not just in need of more information. And it's something of an understatement to say he has information-processing difficulties.

I decided to see how one of the best depth psychologists treats the relation between affect and cognition, or emotion and thought. David Shapiro describes the cognitive fixity and rigidity of the obsessive-compulsive personality and its relation to underlying affect:

> An obsessive compulsive patient — a sober, technically-minded and active man — was usually conspicuously lacking in enthusiasm or excitement in circumstances that might seem to warrant them. On one occasion, as he talked about a certain prospect of his, namely, the good chance of an important success in his work, his sober expression was momentarily interrupted by a smile. After a few more minutes of talking, during which he maintained his soberness only with difficulty, he began quite hesitantly to speak of certain hopes he had only alluded to earlier. Then he broke into a grin. Almost immediately, however, he regained his usual, somewhat worried expression. As he did this, he said, "Of course, the outcome is by no means certain," and he said this in a tone that, if anything, would suggest that the outcome was almost certain to be a failure. After ticking off several of the possibilities for a hitch, he finally seemed to be himself again, so to speak.[11]

It's as though a certain affect, or feeling, in this case joy or enthusiasm, were struggling to the surface against an implacable foe. The affect is unacceptable and *leads* to a series of thoughts that will dampen it, choke it off. Shapiro argues that the feeling of joy is associated in this particular man's mind with exaggeration and loss of control, an "unrealistic" optimism that could bring massive disappointment later. He has learned to control these dangerous feelings with thoughts. His thoughts make the feelings go away. From the outside — the vantage point of cognitivists — his information processing is impoverished, his thought processes, illogical. But to him, they are lifesaving. He clings to them tenaciously. He thinks his logic impeccable and his prudence admirable. Often, he will believe that those who follow their impulses and enthusiasms are dangerous fools.

Most of psychoanalysis and psychiatry is devoted to discovering how this man and others like him got this way. The two professions are concerned with aetiology and treatment. They're concerned with biological and genetic influences, maturational processes and child-rearing practices, all of which are fascinating but not for our purposes here. Further, because they grew within the bosom of the medical model, they are concerned largely with pathology and have precious little to say about creative, positive human productions. And leadership, whether you call it "charismatic," "transformational" or "visionary,"[12] is one of those creative human productions. Thus, while I would carry with me some psychoanalytic baggage — its work on the analysis of character — I was still seeking a terrain that put the Humpty-Dumpty of emotion, thinking and action back together again, but resulted not in pathology but in greatness. I turned to philosophy. Away from Locke and Hume, back to Plato, forward to Kant and Kierkegaard. From Kant to Croce, Santayana and Cassirer, Ruskin, Collingwood and Reid, Merleau-Ponty, Langer and Sparshott. In short, I turned to aesthetics, philosophy of art.

Ruskin wrote that fine art is the domain in which the hand, the head and the heart of man go together, his "finest hour." No one, at least no one in his right mind, would try to pretend that an artist's emotions get in the way of his thoughts and his actions. In aesthetics the whole man — willing, feeling, thinking, acting — is restored to us.

The Nature of Art

The work of aesthetics has been largely classificatory. The art historian finds or creates periods and labels them classical or romantic. Styles are identified: mannerist, impressionist, cubist. There is explication of symbols as the critic seeks to sort the artistic wheat from the mannerist chaff. There is much discussion of technique, the origins and use of devices like perspective. But philosophers, aestheticians, have struggled for millennia to define art, and the intensity of the debate has not cooled in our day.

ART AS REVELATION

If there has been controversy around what constitutes art, there is much more consensus around art's achievements, and indeed its purpose. British aesthetician Sir Herbert Read insists that art has always revealed to us new insights:

> Art, in so far as it has retained its function and not become a matter for pastry cooks, has throughout history always been such a mode of revelation, of establishment, of naming.[13]

The artist, he argues, is an explorer for mankind and the "explorer's fumbling progress is a much finer achievement than the well-briefed traveller's journey.[14] His task is *épater la bourgeoisie*, to break through the limitations of previously codified knowledge, to lead man into his future. Art, believed British painter John Constable, ought to be thought of as a branch of science; it investigates, it reasons. It creates symbols that facilitate thought:

> . . . a symbol is used to articulate ideas of something we wish to think about and until we have a fairly adequate symbolism we cannot think about them.[15]

Language provides that symbol system for discursive logic, but Langer tells us that there are whole domains of experience that philosophers deem "ineffable," or too great for words. Art provides the medium, the language, for the expression of these ineffable thoughts. This may help us to better understand Robert Motherwell, who says, "All my life I've been working on the work — every canvas a sentence or paragraph of it." Or Isadora Duncan, who cried, "If I could say it, I wouldn't have to dance it."[16]

Gombrich, eminent art historian, provides a metaphor:

> The history of art, as we have interpreted it so far, may be described as the forging of master keys for opening the mysterious locks of our senses to which only nature originally held the key. They are complex locks . . . [and] like the burglar who tries to break a safe, the artist has no direct access to the inner mechanism. He can only feel his way with sensitive fingers, probing and adjusting his hook or wire when something gives way. Of course, once the door springs open, once the key is shaped, it is easy to repeat the performance. The next person needs no special insight.[17]

The next person needs no special insight; he may perfect or adapt the insight, as a craftsman does. Or, he may mimic the insight, as a technician or a virtuoso does. In fact, great artists are always followed by a host of imitators — mannerists. Haven't we all seen pseudo-Monets at our local fairs? And pseudoleaders in our organizations?

The true artist's lot, however, is normally not an easy one. The great ones often burn out early, like Gauguin or Rimbaud. Each attempt to forge the key, to unlock the treasure, may be met with an infinite sense of disappointment, depression, even despair. Thus does a Giacometti destroy his sculptures almost immediately after their birth.[18] They fail him. They do not live up to their promise.

ARTISTIC PERCEPTION

Art, writes Sparshott, occupies the ground between "chaos and cliché," and

> artistic activity begins when man grapples with the twisted mass of the visible which presses in upon him and gives it creative form. . . . The true artist cannot acquiesce in this phenomenal chaos.[19]

When we survey today's economic and social landscape, doesn't it seem like "a twisted mass"? Many aestheticians have sought the explanation for art in the perception of artists. For some reason, the artist is viewed as more susceptible to the world, more sensitive to its subtleties, more prone to see chaos where others see order. Some have attributed this partly to heredity, pointing to studies that show artistic activity runs in families.[20] Others have argued that the artist's perception is simply clearer, uncorrupted by concepts of what "should" be seen. Another aesthetician, Roger Fry, concludes:

> Art, then, is, if I am right, the chief organ of the imaginative life . . . and, as we have seen, the imaginative life is distinguished by the greater clearness of its perception, and the greater purity or freedom of its emotion.[21]

Perception is not, of course, simply that which strikes our sense organs. We bring structures to perception, and the explanation of art concerns itself as much with the artist's inner life as with his apparent reactions to the visible world. Here, as Fry notes above, the imagination is king. The artist is someone more attuned to the rhythms of his inner world — imagination, fantasy, dreams. The poet Spender writes that he is "aware of a rhythm, a dance, a fury, which is yet empty of words."[22] Coleridge apparently crafted his dreamlike *Kubla Khan* in a reverie.

The dreamlike quality of art is nowhere more evident than in modern surrealism. Whether it be stream-of-consciousness literature evident in Proust or James Joyce, or in the paintings of a Marc Chagall (see the reproduction below), these works seem to capture not only the fleetingness of dream reality but also the strangeness of its forms and images. Time, space and concept lose their imperious control over shape and substance. Our normal, everyday, conventional ways of seeing things are broken down.

Bennis tells us that one of the characteristics of transformational leaders is that they are adept at "unlearning." In general, great art always seems to involve both destruction and creation — destruction of old forms, old gestalts, in the service of the new, or, as Barron puts it, "the structure of the world must be broken then transcended."[23] Some artists seem to have understood this basic dialectic; listen to Picasso and Schiller:

Marc Chagall, *I and the Village*, 1911. The Museum of Modern Art, New York.

Thus, no less gifted an artist than Picasso confesses that, "a painting moves forward to completion by a series of destructions." And, the poet Schiller wrote, "What would live in song immortally/ must in life first perish."[24]

To suggest that the everyday structure of the world must first be broken and the world of dreamlike images given precedence is not to suggest that art is but a dream or fantasy, a pure product of the unconscious. Consciousness controls the production of the creative product, but it seems to work on a fragment, a hint, a foreshadowing, not directly given to it. This is why the act of creation is anything but the tidy transcription of some prior mental image. It takes work, often agony. Spender says of his own poetic inspiration that there is "but the dim cloud of an idea which I feel must be condensed into a shower of words."[25] Ducasse stresses this open-endedness of art and the fragmentary nature of the inspiration when he writes that "the feeling that the work of art comes to embody may be there only as a germ *ab initio*."[26] More clearly still, French philosopher Merleau-Ponty suggests that because of the fragmentary nature of vision and its inarticulate nature, we never know in advance whether an artistic vision will be "useful" or not. We have to see the finished product:

> There is nothing but a vague fever before the act of artistic expression and only the work itself, completed and understood, is proof that there was *something* rather than *nothing* to be said.[27]

Later we will see that artistic leaders also have trouble explaining their visions and justifying their actions.

If the artistic enterprise is, then, an attempt to build a new intellectual home for man, a new order more suitable to his growing capacities, it must break with the past and shape new forms. To do so, it demands trust and time, two things that today are in short supply.

Finally I was getting somewhere. Vision is the currency of great art and of great leadership. Artists and leaders, and great scientists for

leaders & artists

that matter, are compelled to break with conventional wisdom; as Bronowski says, we expect them to "fly in the face of what is established."[28] But I still needed to know more about how the artist accomplishes his task. I needed to know more about the artist's character. Plato said: "The person who comes to the doors of poetry without madness from the Muses, convinced that technique will have made him an adequate poet, gets nowhere; the poetry of the self-controlled is annihilated by that of the crazed."[29] I already knew that mastering the techniques of modern management didn't make great managers, but did this mean that great artists and visionary leaders were all nuts?

Well, no, not exactly, but they are abnormal in the same sense that someone seven feet tall is abnormal. It is in the emotional domain that they distinguish themselves from equally intelligent but less creative people. They are nonconformist, like complexity and disorder more than others and score much higher on tests of intuition. They are moody. They have a marked tendency to depression on the one hand or to hyperthymia (elevated mood) on the other, or to a cyclic combination the two — cyclothymia. Da Vinci's depressions were legendary. Van Gogh's, lethal. Lord Brain, a British aesthetician, tells us about Charles Dickens, whose moods alternated regularly between elation and despair:

> I have suggested before that Charles Dickens was a cyclothyme. His prevailing mood was one of elation which gave him his enormous gusto and energy which, apart from his prolific inventiveness, was always overflowing into long walks, parties and amateur theatricals. His son, Sir Henry Dickens, speaks of his father's "heavy moods of deep depression, of intense nervous irritability, when he was silent and oppressed." Dickens himself [wrote] "I am sick, giddy and capriciously despondent. . . . I have bad nights, am full of disquietude and anxiety . . . my wretchedness just now is inconceivable."[30]

I expected to discover — indeed some of the leaders I was studying had already said as much — that some great leaders were subject to depression and discouragement. After all, defying conventional wisdom is not

18

an easy job. But, like Dickens, they are also characterized by prolonged periods of immense energy and boundless optimism. The flip side of the cyclothymic character, this provides the drive, the enthusiasm, the force to impose the new vision.

Most people are wedded to the conscious gestalts, or the "cognitive schemas," of everyday life. In general this is good. It keeps us on track. But as Jung reminds us, a track can become a rut without our artists:

> The definiteness and directedness of the conscious mind are extremely important acquisitions which humanity has bought at a very heavy sacrifice, and which, in turn, have rendered humanity the highest service. Without them science, technology, and civilization would be impossible, for they all presuppose the reliable continuity and directedness of the conscious process. . . . We may say that social worthlessness increases to the degree that these qualities are impaired by the unconscious. Great artists and others distinguished by their creative gifts are, of course, exceptions to this rule.[31]

The artist has better access to his imagination, but so does the schizophrenic. Unlike the schizophrenic, however, the artist's conscious faculties are able to control and dominate the flood of imagery and associations originating in the unconscious.[32] Thus, he is able to break with conventional gestalts and ideas and forge new ones, whereas the compulsive personality, so afraid of letting go, has his consciousness dry up into a "banal, empty, arid rationality."[33]

All right. I won't trouble you with any more of this. By now you have enough to go on. The artistic character is quite distinct. I also had got some clues about its opposite, "banal, empty, arid rationality." And along the way, I had learned about craftsmanship.

THE ARTIST IDEAL TYPE

The object of my voyage into the domain of art was to discover the character of the artist and the nature of his enterprise on the assumption that it was not dissimilar to visionary leadership. In 1905 the philosopher George Santayana told us, "Man's progress has a poetic phase in which he imagines the world, then a scientific phase in which he sifts and tests what he has imagined."[34] We depend, as a civilization, on the artist's vision; it is he who forces us, often reluctantly, to change our ways of seeing. His visions stem not from some conscious desire to be rebellious, but from his character. He is peculiarly susceptible to the outer and inner world; he lives, precariously, at their frontier. My search permitted me to construct the Artist Ideal Type, a set of descriptors that might represent, let us say, every artist in general and none in particular. Lord Brain's "administrative artist," I hazarded, would evidence a frustration with conventional wisdom, a willingness, even a need, to depart from it. This would stem from his character, a character that would have a hyper-thymic or cyclothymic base and that would cause him to be subject to bouts of depression and periods of elation. In those periods of elation, he would have lots of ideas. To others, he will seem intuitive, imaginative, unpredictable, volatile, emotional; some may believe he lives in a dream-world.

THE TECHNOCRAT IDEAL TYPE

To see the Artist clearly, we have need of a contrast. When technique is elevated to a first principle, its carrier becomes a Technocrat, "one for whom the technical sides of an issue take precedence over the social and human consequences."[35] If what predominantly character-izes the artistic character is his capacity to alternate between con-sciousness and the unconscious, to live on the frontier without becoming ill, then what characterizes his opposite is that he cannot do so. Above, Rollo May referred to the compulsive character who is so fearful of unconscious contents that his consciousness dries up in "banal, empty, arid rationality." If the Artist is typified by a reaction against conventional wisdom, the compulsive character clings to it, conforms to it, deifies it. In trying to impede the flow of unconscious material, the compulsive succeeds in stultifying all affect, all emotion. In general, he exudes emotional control, even rigidity. Reich called these people "living machines."[36] Machines don't get hunches; the Technocrat will rarely be described as intuitive. What counts for him are the "facts," the "rules," the "right way to do things."

Playfulness is not on the agenda for Technocrats. Spontaneity is ruled out. They are stubborn and will brook no interference with their plans, which are, after all, based on the "facts." Their chief defence mechanism is intellectualization. Because they are most comfortable with detail, with facts, they often evidence technical virtuosity and ingenuity, and this is the source of their power. In management, we need only think of the accomplishments of Frederick Winslow Taylor, his obsessional time-and-motion studies, to see both the virtues and the difficulties of this character pattern. His system was ingenious, but he missed the affective tone of the controversy it engendered. For him, it was simply based on the facts, which were, for him and by definition, emotionally neutral. Of course, facts have no status independent of time and of their observers; it used to be a fact that the world was flat. And a person, or a "society which believes in magic, witchcraft and oracles, will agree on a whole system of 'facts' which modern men regard as fictitious."[37]

THE CRAFTSMAN IDEAL TYPE

If the Artist's visions are "bridges thrown toward an unseen shore,"[38] the Craftsman is the guy who builds the bridges. In an organizational context, Mintzberg has taught us about crafting strategy.[39] In keeping with the work of Lindblom and Quinn, Mintzberg sees strategy formation as a continuous, incremental process, one that necessarily adapts to the continuous demands of an uncertain marketplace. In general, craftsmanship is always *étapist*. It is always about the constant, slow accumulation of knowledge and skill. As noted earlier, the distinction between craft and art continues to provoke considerable debate within aesthetics. When does craft become art? Are they two distinct categories or do they exist on a continuum? These are just some of the questions that plague philosophers. Our interest is not this debate but rather the set of descriptors about craft the debate provides, allowing us to define the Craftsman Ideal Type.

If, with Santayana, we believe that man's progress has a poetic phase, which corresponds to art, and a scientific phase, which, here, corresponds to technique, it also has a craft phase, where what is found with art comes into use and is transformed, perfected, refined, concretized, shaped, sculpted, by experience. It could be argued, for instance, that the French Impressionist painters created a genre in which the Craftsmen, the Canadian Group of Seven, worked. They adapted the peculiar insights of the French to a uniquely Canadian context. Samuel Johnson, the great British satirist, was undoubtedly wrong when he said, "You cannot with all the talk in the world, enable a man to make a shoe."[40] Writing before the triumph of industrialism, he could not foresee that what was then a strong craft could, with time and ingenuity, be transformed into a set of techniques and that machines would one day make shoes. His underlying point, however, about craft remains forceful. Craft is based on lore, a body of traditions.[41] These traditions pass from master to apprentice in an active, physical sense — not in a classroom or a book. You cannot "tell" a man how to make good pottery, a serviceable shoe, a watercolour image that does not run into the next, how to run an organization. These accomplishments require practice, long experience, Michael Polanyi's "tacit knowledge."

Craft is based on practice, and practice is not mere repetition. Practice, apprenticeship, teaches simultaneous doing and thinking. It is conceptual, as well as practical. "The procedures we follow tend to emerge not only from tradition but also from our momentary successes and failures in applying what tradition has given us."[42] Craft is the difference between "knowing" and "understanding"; the craft of singing, for example, is the "science of acoustics [knowing] joined to the experiential understanding of the body [understanding]."[43] Experience is essential to understanding.

Craftsmanship poses deep challenges in our modern world. A respect for the practical sides of any art demands submission to authority because the craft must be transmitted from master to apprentice. Polanyi insists:

> To learn by example is to submit to *authority*. You follow your master because you trust his manner of doing things even when you cannot analyze or account in detail for its effectiveness. . . . A society which wants to preserve a kind of personal knowledge must submit to *tradition*."[44]

Having submitted to learning by doing, we acquire a practical understanding of the art; it cannot be reduced to maxims. Polanyi continues:

> Maxims are rules, the correct application of which is part of the art which they govern. The true maxims of golf or poetry increase our insight into golf or poetry and may even give valuable guidance to golfers and poets; but, these maxims would instantly condemn themselves to absurdity if they tried to replace the golfer's skill or the poet's art. Maxims cannot be understood, still less applied, by anyone not already possessing a good practical knowledge of the art.

Most business schools require that MBA applicants have at least a modicum of experience before admission; this, because they sense that their maxims cannot be understood, still less applied, by anyone not already possessing a good practical knowledge of the art. On the other hand, how often have we been told a set of maxims about how organizations should be managed? And how often have these maxims been offered by people who have never set foot in our organizations? Further, as a society, we don't much like authority or tradition; so, we have a lot of problems with craftsmanship.

If the foregoing presents an adequate portrait of craft, what does it tell us about the organizational Craftsman? For one thing, he will be patient. To submit to authority implies an ability to set aside, temporarily, one's own preferred way of doing things. He will probably be conservative, in the sense of respecting tradition. He will not be quick to depart from the tricks of his trade. He will be frustrated by maxims detached from an understanding made possible only by experience. He will be responsible, sensible and exhibit good judgement. He will be honest, loyal and straightforward. He will be amiable and tolerant.

Well, this has been a rather long-winded attempt to put you into my frame of mind, to show you *what* I was looking for and *why*. My challenge became *how* to take these insights into management, how to study "administrative genius," Artists in action, their fellow travellers, the Craftsmen, and their opposites, the Technocrats.

Previous leadership research has foundered largely on methodological reefs. First, researchers have confounded the position with the person who occupies it and concluded that all leaders are different. But not all people in positions of power are "leaders." Some may have inherited the position. Some may have stolen it. Some may have been compromise candidates. Second, researchers have confounded public reputation with "leadership." I know from bitter experience that many so-called visionary leaders with sterling public reputations do not merit the title: they've inherited the fruits of previous *real* visionaries' work. Finally, researchers have overestimated the value of interviews with "leaders." People dissimulate in interviews and, unless you are a psychiatrist or a psychoanalyst, it's very hard to detect. That's why to get a handle on leaders you have to interview them, to be sure, but you also have to interview their colleagues and subordinates — witnesses. And that takes a long time and multiple methods.

So, with these pitfalls in mind, here's what I expected to find: Artists, great leaders, who would be high on vision and capable of consciously controlling that vision; Technocrats, who would lack vision but would be very much oriented toward control; and Craftsmen, with, let us say, medium-term vision and sufficient control. I didn't expect to find any fools or madmen. No fools get to the top of major organizations. Nor do many madmen.

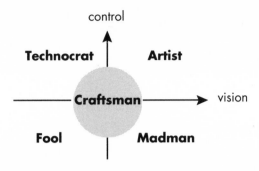

Multiple Methods

What I may call art, someone else may not. Someone I claim is an artist may be seen by others to be a fool or a madman. Somehow I had to develop a set of research tools that would permit me to say certain things with some level of confidence, some level of intersubjective validity. If you're still with me, here is what I did.

For many years, I watched a major international financial-services organization with assets in the tens of billions of dollars and operating divisions on several continents.[45] As a witness at countless board and committee meetings, as well as special sessions, it was plain to me that there were three character types who were involved in the life of the organization at its highest level — the fifteen CEOs of the group as a whole and of its major operating divisions. Each type spoke a different language, had different concerns, different priorities. One group wanted the organization to conquer the world, or at least major parts of it; another wanted to get better and better at doing what it already did; a third wanted to get the "systems" right and produce profit. Of course, both the first two groups also wanted to produce profit, but their definitions or their notions about *how* to produce it differed enormously from the third's. How could I prove that there were indeed three distinct groups, that this was not just my fantasy? Three ways.

I indulged in the North American penchant for measurement. First I constructed something called an adjective checklist (ACL).[46] This list consisted of sixty everyday adjectives like "funny," "serious," "honest," "controlled" and so on. I expected Artists to be seen, among other things, as "intuitive," Craftsmen as "realistic" and Technocrats as "meticulous." In interviews with board members, peers and, in some cases, vice-presidents, I then asked ten observers to fill in these ACLs on each of fifteen key executives. For example, James was the CEO of the group from 1965 to the early 1980s. I asked ten of his closest colleagues — admirers and detractors — to respond to the lists with the instruction "When you think of James, what are the adjectives that spontaneously spring to mind?" The responses were collected and the result was nine thousand (60 adjectives x 10 observers, x 15 executives = 9000) bits of information. I then fed this data into a computer and got some fancy mathematical solutions — factor and correspondence analysis — that told me there were indeed three groups of people (see the Technical Appendix for details).

Appearances can be misleading. This result, while encouraging, was based upon perceptions. What if the perceptions were wrong in some sense? What if the *real* person was different than he seemed to be? To corroborate the adjective story, I needed to know something about the inner world of those fifteen people. Would the inner conform to the outer? So, I administered something called the Minnesota Multiphasic Personality Inventory (MMPI). This is a standard psychological test used every day in literally tens of thousands of clinical diagnostic settings around the world. It is *not* a quick and dirty cute little personality quiz. It is a serious instrument based on 566 questions, and takes several hours to complete. The results of this test were machine scored to guarantee objectivity and interpreted with the assistance of a clinical psychologist from Toronto. The personality profiles that emerged confirmed that I was dealing with a stable and consistent phenomenon. Once again, the three groups emerged.

For the rest, I studied internal and public documents for the thirty-year period 1960 to 1990, with particular concentration on the years 1975 to 1990. In addition to watching, listening and talking, I conducted sixty in-depth interviews with executives and board members — two rounds in 1986 and again in 1990. I asked them about the evolution of the group, its strategy, its structure, its culture, its team spirit.

Let's see what I found.

I

The Players
and the Plot

One The Artist

Ah, but a man's reach must exceed his grasp,
Or, what's a heaven for?

ROBERT BROWNING, ANDREA DEL SARTO

He walks into the room and everyone smiles. Everyone, that is, except the Technocrats. They remain impassive. Sometimes, slight scowls of irritation cross their faces to disappear as rapidly as they came. They resume their serious conversations. Slowly but surely, the others all move toward him, to shake hands, to bask in that broad smile, to be around him, to be affected by his engaging energy and charm. He has a personal word for each one. "How was your trip from Vancouver?" "How's that project you were working on? Is it going well? Can I help?" "How's Mary? Did she get over that flu? Tell her Sally sends her best. We'll be in New York next month and we'll get to see you both." Someone whispers a joke in his ear; he laughs uproariously. Then, almost reluctantly, he says, "Well, I guess we better get down to business."

He is tall, strong, with the flashing eyes that betray the intelligence and vivacity behind them. Around those eyes, fanning out above and below, we see the only lines on his face — laugh lines. His bearing, his silvery grey hair, lend him an air of wisdom and class. Truly a fine example of the male of the species, an aristocrat. But he's not alone. There are two others like him in the room.

One of them is slightly shorter but still very strongly built, tall and broad-chested. He, too, has grey hair. He, too, laughs easily, heartily, and his face bears witness in the form of deep laugh lines running from nose to mouth. But he's more tense, rigid, excitable. He makes me think of a nervous thoroughbred just before the big race. His eyes lack the softness of the first; they are more penetrating, intense. His forehead is deeply creased; there are telltale furrows of stress and fatigue and, maybe, of a hard night before. His greetings are warm — a grin, a brief hug — but shorter in duration, and he has a slightly distracted manner, as though he has a dozen other things on his mind. And he does.

The third one is suave. I know this word has fallen out of use in an age that sees Old World manners in a man as sexist. But suave is the word I want. He's smooth, not in the modern pejorative sense of ingratiating, but smooth in the sense of soft, not abrasive. His smile is genuine and warm. His voice is pleasantly modulated, his chuckle, vaguely seductive. He wants every woman in the room to feel like a queen, especially the older and/or not-so-attractive among them. Some of these women, the brittle ones, bristle on contact. The others primp and preen, feel special. His manner is not intended to manipulate or to condescend. He was raised to be polite and, in his world and in his day, part of being polite was to make a "lady" feel good about herself. This smooth exterior belies the force, the drive, the energy, the determination that lurk below the surface. I'm sure he has often been fatally underestimated by his foes.

These three men are very different. Each was born in a different world, at a different time and a different place. Their family constellations were different: one lost his father very young, one had a happy childhood, one was more troubled. Their educational backgrounds are poles apart: one has a lot of formal education, degrees in both law and business, and two were apprenticed to their trade. One worked all his professional life in the same business; one, half his life; the other has had many different jobs. At lunch with them in January 1994, two and a half years after the completion of my study, I asked them if it felt odd to be lumped into the same sack. "No, not at all," they said. When you respect someone, you don't mind the comparison.

For, in spite of their vast differences, these men are the same. They are leaders, visionary leaders; in my jargon, Artists. Let's call them, respectively, James, Cobb and Mike. Remember, as I explained in the Introduction, I asked ten of their colleagues — friends and enemies — to give me a reading of these three men and twelve others. All those responses were fed into a computer program that gave me a mathematically generated map of all the characters. First, let's zoom in on one part of that map. Later, we'll look at the whole picture. As you can see, James, Mike and Cobb are surrounded by a cloud of adjectives. At the centre are the core adjectives — inspiring, funny, entrepreneurial, visionary, intuitive, emotional. Radiating outwards, we find imaginative, bold, daring, unpredictable, volatile, exciting, people-oriented, easygoing, warm, generous. Barely outside of the outer circle, we pick up open-minded, a quality they share with the Craftsmen.

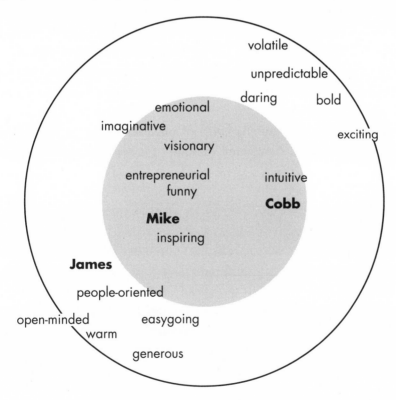

Without getting into the mathematics, let me try to explain what this means. Just because the word "inspiring" sits next to Mike does not mean that Mike is the most inspiring of the three. The position of any person or any adjective is determined jointly by the mathematical impact of every other adjective or person. In the computer algorithm, these particular adjectives and people were "fighting" other adjectives and people; for example, "open-minded" was mathematically drawn to both the Artist and the Craftsman and therefore ended up in the core area of neither. The cluster of adjectives we see here represents what I call the Artist Ideal Type. Real people diverge from this Ideal Type by degrees. The adjective "exciting," for example, is highly correlated with the adjective "bold" and more weakly correlated with the adjective "warm" but James is exciting and warm. It's all a matter of degrees. The farther you get out from the core, the less the person conforms to the archetype. James, for instance, shares many qualities of the Craftsman, which we will explore in the next chapter. Collectively these adjectives are signposts or, if you will, the fingerprint of the visionary leader. Remember, they were produced by people who liked them and people who despised them.

There are very different kinds of qualities going on here. Let's take them in groups: behaviour, thought processes and temperament.

BEHAVIOUR

This group might loosely be called action, or behaviour, words: entrepreneurial, bold, daring, unpredictable, exciting. Unpredictable, because the *design* is only in *their* heads — not on paper. An occasion comes along to complete a piece of the design so they seize it: *carpe diem!* They're entrepreneurial. To the outside world, this may look to be, at best, opportunism and at worst, madness, but in all cases it is unpredictable. It will also seem bold and daring because it is very apt to defy conventional wisdom of the day: a camera does not take "instant" pictures (Polaroid); a computer is never "friendly" (Macintosh); "family" doesn't go with sports car (Mustang) nor "sovereignty" with "association" (René Lévesque). For Pete's sake, these things just aren't done! In this world, the world of James and Mike and Cobb, the equivalent was "Banks simply do not buy cable companies." But they don't like to bow to conventional wisdom. So, they create excitement.

Thought Processes

Then there are what you might call qualities of the mind or thought processes: imaginative, visionary, intuitive, open-minded. One of James's longtime associates, a woman, said of him:

> I was always astonished and puzzled by his capacity to sense the waves of the future before anyone else. Sometimes I thought of it as feminine intuition; the French call it *pif*, the nose for it. Like some kind of sixth sense.

This is common to all the responses to these men. They think very long-term. Cobb talks about strategy:

> To develop a strategy you have to have a vision. I have a vision for twenty years, but then I have to bring my vision down to five years and to three . . . You work backwards to strategy. It can't be born out of day-to-day perception.

Is it based on gathering all the right facts? I asked him.

> The strategy comes from astrology, quirks, dreams, love affairs, science fiction, perception of society, some madness probably, ability to guess. It's clear but fluid. Action brings precision. Very vague but becomes clear in the act of transformation. Creation is the storm.

Doesn't this remind you of the poet Spender, who told us earlier of his own poetic inspiration that there was only "the dim cloud of an idea which I feel must be condensed into a shower of words"? And Merleau-Ponty who told us that "there is only a vague fever before the act of artistic creation and only the work itself, completed and understood, is proof that there was *something* rather than *nothing* to be said." Cobb tells us that this vague, indefinable, long-term vision is clarified only in action and, he later adds, by remaining open to new insights.

Why, then, do people follow these guys if they have no idea where they're going? I would argue that they do know where they're going, but it's vague, more a trip than a destination. If you ask a great painter what he's going to paint next, it's a rare one who will have a detailed answer and if he does, I doubt he satisfies the definition of "great." Studies show that better artists stay radically open as they work on a canvas; there is a continuous interaction between a vague vision and the concrete act of painting. Visionary leaders inspire with metaphors rather than with detailed descriptions of the future. James talked repeatedly, in the early days, of a branching tree. According to his contemporaries, these metaphors had to be decoded.

Since, we are always told, a picture is worth a thousand words, let me economize a little on the words. I claim that the visions of the visionary leader are no different in form or origin that those of an artist. Take the following reproduction of a painting by Salvador Dali. You can't tell me that Dali had a clear mental picture of this painting *before* he painted it. All of aesthetics tells us otherwise. Now look at the graphic following it. This is my attempt to capture James's metaphor of the branching tree, which for him way back in the 1960s, sitting in a small regional capital of the western world, meant something about a major international, integrated, financial-services company *at least twenty years before* such a strategy became a modern, conventional notion.

James had a *design*, but it was inchoate, unclear, fragmentary, "nothing but a germ *ab initio*" and only in *his* head. How could it be

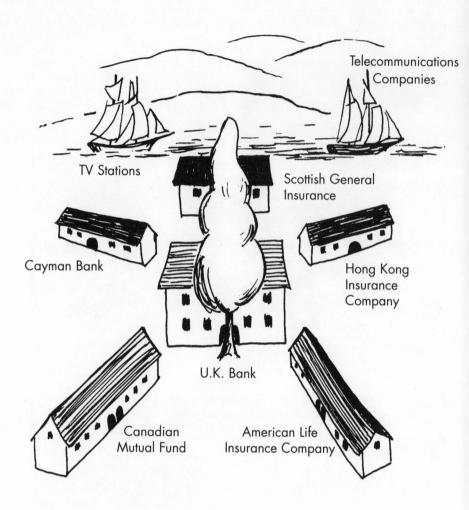

Telecommunications Companies

TV Stations

Scottish General Insurance

Cayman Bank

Hong Kong Insurance Company

U.K. Bank

Canadian Mutual Fund

American Life Insurance Company

otherwise? Conceptually it didn't exist, and at the time, the conventional wisdom was "Bankers are bankers and insurers are insurers and never the twain shall meet": the so-called four pillars of the financial world (banking, trust, insurance and brokerage) were each inviolable. To complete his "painting," he needed time and power. Artists are notoriously jealous of their artistic control. Imagine someone having the power to say to Dali, halfway through the work, "That silly-looking tree in the centre doesn't make sense; take it out." Each piece of the dream that James put together — from a U.K. bank to a Canadian mutual fund to cable companies on the horizon, ostensibly unrelated to financial services — was, for him, indispensable to the design, although he could not have articulated it beforehand. So he talked in metaphors and seized occasions and was accused of opportunism, working without a plan.

Artistic vision always seems to have this fragmentary quality. Beethoven is said to have composed the whole of the *Hammerclavier Sonata* beginning with a point of rupture between two broad movements that had yet to be conceived.[1] In a letter to his mother, Mark Twain describes such a phenomenon:

> I am trying to think out a short story. I've got the closing sentence of
> it all arranged and it is good and strong, but I haven't got any of the
> rest of the story yet.[2]

How do you explain to a nonbeliever that you indeed have an idea for a short story, a sonata, a strategic vision for your organization? Discursive logic, language, is inadequate to the task, but a metaphor might do it.

And, to come back to my main theme of why people followed them, now we have a vision and it's wedded to action, fast action, exciting action, death-defying high-wire acts. This is already enough to cause people to sit up and take notice and for some to wish to follow. Coupled with the other group of qualifiers, you have a knockout. These are, let us say, the qualities of the heart, of temperament.

T EMPERAMENT

People-oriented, easygoing, warm, generous, funny, emotional and volatile. I began this chapter talking about how James came into the room and always, without fail, had a warm personal word for everyone. To be sure, he was also task-oriented and extremely busy, but not so busy as to ignore people. James and Mike and Cobb are all people-oriented, not in the sense of being preoccupied with how to motivate them, but in the sense that they take people, their feelings, their needs, their worries and fears, into account. All is not a calculus. Cobb talks about charisma:

> I always believed that a work environment is fun if it has a drive, it has a sense of purpose, a sense of making people feel that they're important, they're achieving something. So I think it was instilling that. . . . It's a simple message, but it strikes down deep in the heart of people and in their feelings. . . . All of a sudden you have allowed them to bring out their emotions, what they feel deep down which never in business are they allowed to do otherwise. . . . That's probably what charisma's all about. Charisma is not about things. Charisma is something of the soul. And because I was bringing it out, others could bring it out and it was contagious, and this is why people were so excited. They were having fun in what they were doing and the pleasure comes, I think, from the fact that your soul is part of the game as well as your mind.

And James dared to say publicly:

> Man reacts instinctively to the pressures of material need and the desire to live in friendship and love. It seems to us that to respond to these twin needs gives our institution a worthy reason for being.

How many CEOs do you know who write about *love* in their annual reports? And how many really believe in a moral purpose for their organizations? One of my Artists talked about the insurance business. His words may surprise you:

I tell my men that they are in the most moral business in the world. Nobody likes to think about death, talk about death. The life-insurance salesman who gets his foot in the door to sell you a life policy is engaged in a moral battle. There are millions of widows and children all over the world who live a better life because some pain-in-the-neck sold a policy to an irritated father.

Add a drop of "generous" and "easygoing" to this curious mixture. What do generous and easygoing mean? They mean you don't get fired if you make one mistake. Let's listen to Cobb again:

> You have to learn to have confidence in your people, to allow them to run, take some chances on them. I kept saying, we have to accept that we're going to make mistakes.

Finally, I've come to the last two adjectives: emotional and volatile. I've left them to the last on purpose, because they are going to allow me to tell another part of the story — the story about the inner life of the Artist. I'm going to tread very softly here because I know a lot of people get uncomfortable when someone talks about psychodynamic principles. Why, a few actually run out of the room at the very mention of Freud or Jung! Hold on. Stay with me. It's important.

Before I get deeply into this, I have to clarify a couple of things. First, I will say nothing about any single individual by name here; such information is entirely too personal and, therefore, out of bounds. Second, I'm adding two other people — Bill and Ross — with artistic leanings (see Technical Appendix) to the artistic group to further protect anonymity.

Okay. Remember the MMPI, the Minnesota Multiphasic Personality Inventory? Five hundred and sixty-six questions machine-scored? It, along with my observations of a decade and the results of all my interviews, forms the basis of this next section.

Inner Life

Man was made for Joy and Woe;
And when this we rightly know
Thro' the World we safely go.

William Blake, Auguries of Innocence

Emotional. Volatile. Joy and Woe. Up and down in both directions. Like Lincoln, Churchill, Dickens and Monet. Churchill called his depressions "the black dog"; they haunted him, stalked him. Charles Dickens told us earlier, "I am sick, giddy and capriciously despondent . . . I have bad nights, am full of disquietude and anxiety . . . my wretchedness just now is inconceivable." And yet, his prevailing mood, the dominant one, was one of elation and energy and prolific inventiveness. So, for the most part, it's joy and excitement these Artists convey, openly and without apology.

To set the stage a little for what follows, let's take a closer look at Winston Churchill. Recognized as visionary even by his enemies, Churchill, as a military strategist, acted on intuitions. (Of course, since intuitions can be as radically wrong as right, he had major failures as well as successes.) He was eloquent and funny and regularly used metaphors to convey his ideas; it is to him we owe the post–World War II expression "iron curtain." His sentences were not marked by rigour or by logic but by metaphor and passion. Before World War II, he mercilessly harangued the British public, warning of the dire consequences of a lack of military preparedness. Listen to the metaphor:

> I have watched this famous island descending incontinently, fecklessly, the stairway which leads to a dark gulf. It is a fine broad stairway at the beginning, but after a bit the carpet ends. A little farther on there are only flagstones, and a little farther still these break beneath your feet.

How much more powerful, more mobilizing, is this image than the comparable "logical" expression: "We are devoting only 2.1 percent of the GNP to preparedness while our potential adversaries have, since 1934, devoted 2.13 and 2.16." Who cares?

Churchill's thirst for adventure, his excitement, even jubilation, was the normal face of the man, but there was also a somber side, the depressions that typify the manic-depressive. While manic-depression, or in medical language, "bi-polar affective disorder,"[3] is a serious illness of genetic and physiological base involving hallucinatory episodes, flight of ideas and complete loss of contact with reality, its more mild form — cyclothymia — was certainly evident in Churchill.[4]

No one is clear about the relationship between depression and creativity, but some argue that all the evidence indicates that the deep experience embodied in a classical work of art, for example, must have been what is clinically called a depression and that the stimulus to create such a perfect whole must have lain in the drive to overcome an unusually strong depression.[5] The temporary loss of interest in the external world, characteristic of depression, may provoke intense activity in the inner world. Apart from its genetic and physiological base, what might provoke the depression? Arieti, a psychiatrist who has made a serious study of the thought processes characteristic of Artists, speculates that the creative person senses a defect, or incompleteness, in the usual ways of looking at the world and finds them suffocating. He needs to break with conventional wisdom. After all, to knock your head repeatedly against the brick wall of complacency is depressing. I asked one of my Artists, "If you could do it all over again, what would you change?" Listen to what he said:

> If I could rewrite my life? Then, the shackles of my youth, I would *smash* them. I would really *destroy* them to allow myself to explore my life.

Conventional limits — what to think, what school to go to, how to behave — all these were unbearable to him. I asked him what kind of people made him uneasy. He replied instantly:

Ambassadors [uproarious laughter]. Because they're phonies . . . And unctuous people. And the cocksure who think they're so much superior to others. The snobs — the snobbier they are the emptier are their heads. The people who have nothing to say. I don't mean the people who are silent. It's people who are so shallow, empty, vain.

In short, the people who mouth clichés and pretend to have ready answers. Conventional wisdoms of all sorts. Pierre Péladeau, a Quebecker who, starting with a small community newspaper in Montreal, now controls an international printing empire with assets of $3 billion (including America's second-largest printer and France's Fécomme), is manic-depressive, takes lithium to control it and has never bowed to conventional wisdom in his life.

All right. There is, for whatever reason — genetic, biological, developmental or circumstantial — a connection between depression and creativity, but the dominant mood is enthusiasm. James wrote:

> Our era demands much but promises even more! Even though we may feel a certain vertigo faced with all the dangers, we can also taste — even exalt in — the joys of knowing, creating, living.

A zest for life in spite of its difficulties and dilemmas — maybe even *because* of them. All these Artists evidence and transmit enthusiasm, but what about this depression business? Let's take a closer look.

The word "depression" is encrusted with all kinds of connotations and superstitions. While some people escape it entirely — the hypermanic — depression is normal. Almost all of us have bad days, sad days, days when we just don't want to do anything. This is mild depression. But depression can wear many faces. It can show itself as a certain lassitude or fatigue or withdrawal, instead of sadness. It can show itself as giddiness, a so-called "smiling depression." Or as an alcohol dependency. It can show itself as hyperactivity; the person is unable to rest or even to sit down for fear that, in doing so, the "black dog" will attack. The artistic personality, the cyclothymic, simply has an intensification of these normal cycles. Whereas when I'm depressed I might go out and buy a new pair of shoes, a manic might go out and buy the Empire State Building and charge it on his Visa. A cyclothymic might come up with all sorts of schemes.

All five of my Artists show up hyperthymic, manic and/or cyclothymic. One of them told me:

> Oh, sure. I've had bouts of depression all my life. Serious depression. But then I just went out and bought another company. It worked every time.

They have rich inner fantasy lives, which they allow themselves to experience. Listen to the blind, clinical interpretation of the MMPI results for one of them:

> Healthy ego. Highly artistic, creative. At times has a hard time distinguishing reality from fantasy. Uses fantasy to overcome anxiety. Exceptionally sensitive, nontraditional male. Quite isolated but has enough energy to interact socially. Quite hysterical. Exceptionally creative and fanciful. Similar to Picasso. Totally nontraditional.

Several important things are going on here. First of all, "healthy ego"; does this mean narcissistic? Not at all. It means strong character, a character capable of living with ambiguity, ambivalence and doubt, neither succumbing to dogmatism nor flying off in an unreal world. According to their psychological profiles based on the MMPI, artists are typically and paradoxically both sicker and healthier than ordinary mortals. They are sicker in the sense of being bombarded by ideas and fantasies; healthier in the sense of being able to control the process and shape something new and useful out of it. The way Edwin Land (of Polaroid fame) describes his process of invention is a good illustration (the emphases are mine):

> I find it very important to work intensively for long hours when I am beginning to see solutions to a problem. At such times *atavistic*

competences seem to come welling up. You are handling so many variables at a *barely conscious* level that you can't afford to be interrupted. If you are, it may take a year to cover the same ground you could otherwise cover in sixty hours.[6]

Secondly, returning to our group, "At times has a hard time distinguishing reality from fantasy. Uses fantasy to overcome anxiety"; does this mean looney tunes? Sort of. But not really. Have you ever noticed that some people dream in technicolour and some in black and white? That some people don't ever seem to have dreams, awake or asleep? That some people literally *hate* dreamers? A rich fantasy life is not synonymous with madness, though it may be the kind of madness Plato associated with the poet. We have to be able to conjure up a new world if we are then to create it. Or, as Santayana told us, "Man's progress has a poetic phase in which he imagines the world and a scientific phase in which he sifts and tests what he imagines."

Two of these men showed significant degrees of autism in their MMPI profiles. Fantasy. Living in a world of one's own. Thus, the frequent solitariness of these men. But if the world is too much for them, if their days are always absorbed by pressing concerns, when can they think? They need, periodically, to get away from the noise and the bustle, if only in their heads.

They are all nonconformists. But not nonconformists in the superficial sense of dress — they dress conservatively — or in the causes they espouse. They are nonconformist in the deeper sense, in the sense of scepticism of all conventional and popular ways of thinking, modern or ancient. They take almost nothing for granted. They are, therefore, radically open to new thought, to new associations and combinations, which some feel to be the *sine qua non* of creativity, like, again, "sports car" and "family," or "instant" and "photography."

To summarize, my Artists are emotional and sometimes moody, volatile and funny. They are nonconformist and frustrated by gospel with a small "g." These characteristics, features of their basic psychological functioning, mean that to the outside world they appear imaginative, intuitive and visionary. Behaviourally, they are daring, adventurous and entrepreneurial and, therefore, for some, exciting. In addition, they like people, so they are "inspiring." Feeling or temperament, thought processes and behaviour come, as I tried to emphasize earlier, in packages. The package is character in this case, the Artist character.

The Artist Character

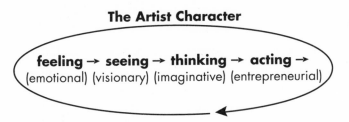

feeling → seeing → thinking → acting →
(emotional) (visionary) (imaginative) (entrepreneurial)

How could we have imagined that someone who is *not* moody and volatile and emotional could be taught to be intuitive and visionary and entrepreneurial? It's a mystery to me.

You may have already guessed what the Artist's Achilles' heel is, but you'll have to wait until Part II. Because now we are going to turn to his fellow traveller, the Craftsman, with whom he has a mutual admiration society.

Two | The Craftsman

His mind was great and powerful, without being of the very first order; his penetration was strong, though not so accurate as that of a Newton, Bacon or Locke; and, as far as he saw, no judgment was ever sounder. Perhaps the strongest feature in his character was prudence. . . . His integrity was most pure, his justice the most inflexible I have ever known. . . .

THOMAS JEFFERSON'S DESCRIPTION OF GEORGE WASHINGTON[1]

Calm, inflamed by injustice or obtuseness. Steady. Solid. Reasonable. Wise. Measures his words. Illustrates his principles with real-life stories. Listens. Weighs. Pauses. Having a conversation with him is a pleasure, a genuine, honest-to-God pleasure. He does not begin with "Okay, what do you want to know?" He doesn't presume to know anything perfectly and can't imagine why I want to talk with him. He's not a theoretical man, and because he thinks I'm a theoretical woman, he thinks he'll have nothing to say. In fact, he has a lot to say, but you have to learn to read between the lines as he recounts seemingly mundane events: "So I told him that he'd make a great consultant but that, as a manager, he was a complete washout." Pretty run-of-the-mill stuff, no? Trouble is, the man he was talking about was his boss. So was the man he was talking *to*.

When I first starting thinking about the Craftsman, my guiding metaphor was a carpenter. I like wood. It feels nice. There's this man who built our house. His name is Gaëtan Roy, and he's a carpenter.

He's had a key to our house for the past eight years (he's very trust-worthy). He whistles while he works, even on Sunday at midnight because he promised (he's very reliable) the job would be done. He likes what he does and he's done it all his life.

"Gaëtan, can we use pine on the floors?"

"You won't like it. It's too soft. I can get a better deal on spruce and it will stand up better."

He's direct. He's economical.

"Gaëtan, can you have those logs cut to make a facing on that wall?"

Sceptical frown. "I don't think so, but I'll ask the guys at the mill."

He doesn't pretend to know everything. He is not embarrassed by this.

"What do I owe you?"

"I logged forty-two hours."

"Here's your money."

He's honest. I don't have to check up on him.

"Gaëtan, I love what you did in the staircase."

"It took me a while to figure it out."

He's modest, humble about his inventiveness but proud of his product.

In general, craftsmanship is about three things: pride, skill and quality. I can't say it better than philosopher Harold Osborne who wrote, in the *British Journal of Aesthetics*, that craftsmanship

> involves a genuine pride in the process of production itself, a pride which drives a man to make whatever he makes as well as they can be made, even beyond the economic considerations of reward. This impulse, which lies at the roots of fine craftsmanship, is now recog-nized by anthropologists to have existed from the earliest stages of human activity. . . . It is this impulse, this cult of excellence, which through the centuries of prehistory and history led to the perpetua-tion of traditions of craftsmanship, the rich storehouses of know-how and skill.

There's a lot going on here. "Pride in the process itself"; isn't this a lot like the old saying "If it's worth doing, it's worth doing well"? This is an instinct that is basic to the Craftsman. He doesn't require college courses on the subject. "The rich storehouses of know-how and skill"; people, Craftsmen in particular, are the rich storehouses, the carriers, of skill and know-how, savoir-faire. What is skill anyway and how do you get it? The dictionary defines skill as "practiced ability"; skilful as "adroit"; skilled as "not untrained or amateur." Adroit, of course, means having dexterity, with its heavy connotations of physical, manual operations. All these denotations and connotations have to do with experience, accumulated, hands-on experience. The Craftsman is proud to use his accumulated skills to produce a high-quality product. He's not an amateur.

Craftsmanship has also to do with the difference between using a tool and using a machine. With a tool, man controls production from start to finish. There is no radical separation between thinking and doing, planning and executing. Unlike a machine, a tool leaves small irregularities and imperfections that cause each product to differ slightly from every other. Each wood — pine, cherry, walnut, mahogany — reacts differently to the tool. Over many years you acquire powers of differentiation and the skills that match them. Osborne continues:

> In general terms, both tools and machines are devices for facilitating man's constant business of adapting his environment to his needs and improving his conditions of life. We speak of "tools" when we mean devices for extending the powers of the organism for manipulating its environment. A part of craftsmanship consists in a man's understanding the tools of his trade, possessing the skill and dexterity to use them to best advantage. . . . A good craftsman, it is said, does not blame his tools. . . . It is a sign of good craftsmanship to know the right tools for the job and to know how to use them. This distinguishes the true craftsman from the amateur.

I like to think of managerial ideas such as total quality management or reengineering as the tools, and employees as the wood (give my metaphor a chance — I don't mean that employees are blockheads). Each circumstance and each employee reacts differently to the tool, so you need a different tool for each. There is no universal tool for all people and all circumstances. Tools are not machines. The Craftsman differentiates, judges, selects the appropriate one according to the wood and the time and the goal. If things go wrong, he doesn't blame the tool or the wood; he blames himself and his own faulty judgement. You do not become a Craftsman overnight. And you cannot just read up on it. You have to *do* it. Now, let's look at the organizational craftsmen.

There are six of them. They all look different. Like the artists, they are different ages and have different educational backgrounds — accountants, MBAs, historians, apprentices and one PhD — the best schools in the world or none at all. They come from different cultures — British, American, Canadian, Quebecker, Scot. They have slight temperamental differences, but in some fundamental sense, they are the same.

Look at the following map. Here's how they are seen. In the core, we find, literally piled upon one another, stable, realistic, reasonable, trustworthy, sensible, polite, responsible, thoughtful, predictable, steady and well-balanced. To the west, conventional; moving northward, controlled and conservative, punctual, hardworking, knowledgeable; turning east and then south, straightforward, dedicated, honest, wise, amiable, helpful, humane and open-minded. Who wouldn't want such a profile? Can you imagine one of these guys rushing out one day to buy a Corvette and leaving his wife and kids to hitch up with some cute young thing? Not on your life. Can you imagine him experiencing a sudden conversion to anything? How do you think he feels about managerial fads?

To get the flavour of these men, we'll go through the same exercise we performed for the Artists; that is, we'll group those adjectives that seem to speak to different issues — behaviour, thought processes and temperament.

49

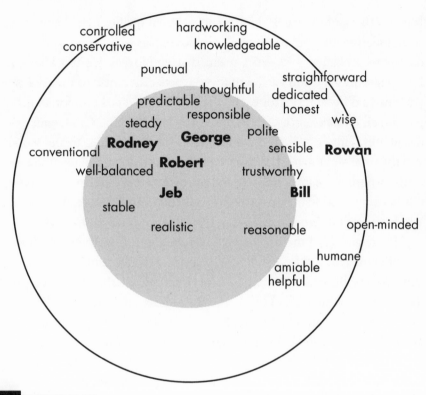

BEHAVIOUR

The adjectives are hardworking, dedicated, predictable, helpful, humane, polite and punctual. He works hard; long hours if there's something urgent, regular hours (say, ten-hour days) if there's not. He'll do whatever he himself judges necessary for the institution — he's dedicated to its success — but it will be his *decision*, his *judgement*. Not a rule. He doesn't stay at his desk on Saturday just to impress someone with his diligence. His behaviour is predictable; you can count on him to be where he says he'll be, doing what he says he'll be doing. He seldom surprises anyone. He's never erratic.

To accomplish his work, he has to work through and with others, and so he's helpful to them. Like master to journeyman, he's humane but firm — "No, that's not how it's done. Try again." He doesn't have a screaming fit if someone makes a mistake. He expects mistakes; one told me, "It takes time to weld a team together and to solve human problems. They're not machines you can just turn on and off." Because he respects others, he is polite and punctual. He wouldn't dream of keeping people waiting for him, because he doesn't want to send the message that he is more important than they are. He is not narcissistic. Let's go to the next level.

THOUGHT PROCESSES

The adjectives are knowledgeable, thoughtful, realistic, sensible, wise, open-minded, conventional and conservative. Knowledgeable. Five out of six of these men (one is a very recent recruit) have worked in the same industry all their lives. This is unsurprising; Osborne tells us, "The old craftsman possessed a hard-won skill derived from lifelong immersion in a centuries-old tradition involving inarticulate knowledge of materials and tools, inherited skills and dexterities, principles of design and pride in excellence." When you meet them they say, "I'm an insurer," or, "I'm a banker." They *don't* say, "I'm in banking," as if to add "right now." They are identified with their traditions. They are proud of them. And they have an intimate knowledge of what those traditions are, how they have evolved and why, though some of this knowledge will be inarticulate tricks of the trade.

Realistic and sensible. I put these two together to come up with a third — good judgement. Why do we call someone or something or some behaviour realistic or sensible. Well, let's see. When we say, "*sensible* shoes," we mean comfortable, useful, practical for walking. We are trying to draw a distinction between them and, say, shoes that are flashy or for a party. So, there's a connotation of appropriateness to the word "sensible." Take another instance. "I wanted to go to Tahiti," says a friend, "but given the state of my bank account, I decided on Florida."

51

We respond with "That was *sensible.*" What do we mean? I think we mean conscious of limits, in this case limits to our debt capacity. Now, we might have said, "That was *realistic,*" but it seems to me that "realistic" carries another connotation. As the root of the word implies, this time we are talking about something conforming to what is *real,* true, actual, not an illusion. I would like to be a ballerina, but at forty-four, the idea is no longer realistic; the mind is willing, but the flesh, oh the flesh . . . If we put all of this together — appropriateness, practicality, limits, conforming to reality — I think we get good judgement.

If we put good judgement together with realistic and sensible and couple it with knowledgeable, we get wise. The dictionary defines wisdom as "*Experience* and *knowledge* together with sagacious *judgement*" (my italics). Young people are rarely wise; wisdom's one of the few advantages of age — because wisdom takes time and lots and lots of experience, and even then, it's not guaranteed. Time is a necessary but insufficient condition. Some people never get wise, either because they forget the past or because they live only in the future, or both. As Santayana told us, in *The Life of Reason,* "Progress, far from consisting in change, depends on retentiveness. Those who cannot remember the past are condemned to repeat it." They are incapable of learning from experience. Or because they never stay in any one place or at any one thing long enough to acquire experience. They are gadflies. Or dilettantes. In any case, the Craftsman is wise enough to know that the past has a heavy impact on the present and the future.

His visions are realistic and, therefore, of medium range, backward and forward in time. He knows where he's come from, and where he's going. He sees the landscape accurately, and he can see to the top of the next hill but not into the valley beyond. His dreams are anchored in the present and the very near future. If we look again at the Dali painting and we put the Craftsman's product beside it, what would it look like? The first change is that the far distant horizon is no longer visible, although the overall form or configuration of the design remains the same. Craftsmen like to keep the structural integrity of the

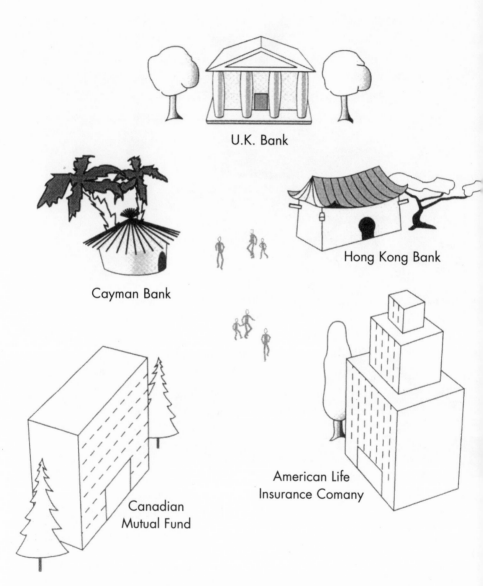

U.K. Bank

Cayman Bank

Hong Kong Bank

Canadian
Mutual Fund

American Life
Insurance Comany

design. They believe in stability; ordinary people, they think, need to be able to trust the map in order to orient themselves. Second, there are more people and trees in the design; it is more lifelike, more realistic. Finally, the buildings all have different shapes; the Craftsman is not wedded to uniformity — different tools, different woods.

Then we come to three confusing adjectives: conservative, conventional, open-minded. They may seem contradictory, but I want you to think of these three words on a continuum that reads something like "Change if necessary but not necessarily change." All craftsmen work within a tradition, and tradition involves a certain inertia. Where the weight of the past is very strong, in Catholicism, for example, change comes more slowly; the inertia is strong. Where the tradition is newer, rock music for example, change may be more rapid; the inertia is weaker. Some individuals will be more open to questioning a tradition than others. And it may depend on the situation or the subject — I may be very traditional about men taking out the garbage, but very open-minded about child care. Craftsmen range across this continuum, sometimes conventional in their approach, sometimes all the way to conservative, then back to open-minded. Pushed, they shove, become stubborn, dig in their heels. Coaxed, they listen. Stimulated, they open up. On questions of principle or morality, they can be, like George Washington, downright pigheaded.

TEMPERAMENT

The adjectives are straightforward, honest, responsible, amiable, stable, well-balanced, steady and controlled. Take straightforward and honest — Jeb, the Craftsman I mentioned earlier who told his boss he would make a great consultant but was a lousy manager. He didn't say this to be cute or provocative, or insulting or insubordinate. He saw it, believed it and said it — naively maybe, but honestly. No games. No duplicity. Straightforward. What you see is what you get.

For the most part amiable, stable and calm, the Craftsman becomes stiffer, more and more intransigent, if his strongly held beliefs are threatened. Like open-minded and conservative, amiable and controlled exist on a continuum, with some Craftsmen in some circumstances more conservative and controlled than they are amiable and open-minded.

All of these qualities add up to trustworthy. Craftsmen are reliable and honest, mostly predictable, always sensible, always realistic, and everybody trusts them. They inspire that magical word "loyalty," because they exhibit it themselves. People are not "excited" to work *for* them; they are pleased to work *with* them. Some people.

INNER LIFE

It's tempting to describe the Craftsman's inner life as zip, zilch, *nada*, *rien*, but that's not true. Only in comparison with the rich fantasy life of the Artist do such words appear to be true. Basically the Craftsman looks like Everyman. Here's a typical interpretation of the MMPI material:

> This must be a Craftsman. Very flat [curve]. Soft, gentle, introspective guy. Just allows the world to happen. No big bitches with the world. Likes people.

This happens to be one of the gentler Craftsmen, but they all share this bit about "no big bitches with the world." They don't have chips on their shoulders. Overall, they like life, find it rewarding. And their mood is usually one, not of buoyancy, but of calm, measured optimism. They expect things to work out in the end. There is actually experimental evidence that so-called normal people wear slightly rose-coloured glasses. Apparently we are all born with an optimism thermometer — it's hard-wired — and at birth the normals have theirs set ever-so-slightly too high.[2] It's as though someone up there knew that life was going to be pretty tough on us.

"Likes people"; are we talking about some gushing sentimentalist? Not at all. Craftsmen fire people. They fire lazy people because lazy people demoralize the responsible ones. They fire people who are insubordinate; they believe in hierarchy and authority. They are *not* authoritarian, but the idea that the apprentice should be master to the master craftsman is a contradiction in terms, illogical, unrealistic, silly. They are pitiless with chronic rebels who are more interested in contesting authority than in getting the job done.[3] But they don't *like* to fire people; they are not sadistic. Nor do they draw some kind of macho pride from it. Bill said to me:

> That S.O.B. [his boss] called me up the other day and his first words were, "How many people have you fired today?" I hung up. It's *disgusting*.

He found it disgusting because, for the Craftsman, people do not just represent costs; they represent the future capacities of the organization. Bill, in his words, "hides" money in his balance sheet. "It's buried so deep they'll never find it; only *I* can find it. That's what I use to develop *my* people." (If the "my" in that sentence resonates with paternalism, that's because it *is* paternalistic; I, for one, think it's good.) Another one, Rodney, told me:

> People are the organization's most important asset. And the institution was important. People like to feel that they're part of something important, have a sense of belonging, *pride*.

Neither the institution nor its employees have a purely instrumental value for Craftsmen; they don't use them to attain some other goal, such as personal prestige or power. The institution has intrinsic value.

Craftsmen are not particularly emotional. In fact, the best description might be "reserved"; there are few displays of emotion. They are very far from being sentimentalists, but they *do* take people into account. They pay attention to them. They invest time in them. And they *do* like to be challenged. Another Craftsman told me about a former vice-president who had been fired. The VP was a difficult guy, but very bright. "He spoke his mind. I'd pay anything to have a guy like that around. He keeps you honest. He didn't agree with you all the time."

Craftsmen know themselves. They know they are not particularly visionary — their vision is medium-term — but that doesn't depress or diminish them. They like themselves. They know their own limits and their own strengths. They are as realistic about themselves as they are about business and life in general. They like the Artists and think every organization needs them. One told me:

> Profit comes from the vision and the people. James and Cobb had the vision. . . . [If you have the vision] and you look after the people, the profit follows. You can't drive at it directly.

The Craftsman works easily with the Artist, chuckles at his histrionics, is sometimes frustrated by his lack of attention to detail, but "would pay anything to have a guy like that around." This, then, is the craft package, the Craftsman character.

The Craftsman Character

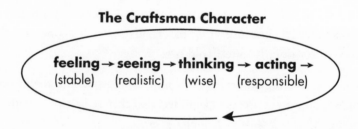

Once again I ask how could we have imagined that someone who is stable and realistic and wise and responsible could, or should, be taught to be passionate, spontaneous, intuitive, a so-called visionary leader?

I'm going to leave the last words of this chapter to Osborne, because his are better than mine. He's talking about craft in general:

> If the craftsmen who are still active in the world can do something to maintain the cult of excellence, the pride in a good job well done, and

the respect for quality, then indeed their contribution to contemporary society is more than justified. They are no *anachronism* but one of the few forces that are left to stem the deterioration and dehumanization of contemporary life. . . . And over the whole field of craftsmanship there is aesthetic delight in the appreciation of skilled and devoted workmanship applied economically to the successful achievement of a practical purpose, while *virtuosity* deployed for its own sake arouses the same sort of distaste as any other form of self-display.

We are now going to meet the virtuoso, who *does* feel that craft is an anachronism.

Three | The Technocrat

"Oho, now I know what you are. You are an advocate of Useful Knowledge."

"Certainly."

"Well, allow me to introduce myself to you as an advocate of Ornamental Knowledge. You like the mind to be a neat machine, equipped to work efficiently, if narrowly, and with no extra bits or useless parts. I like the mind to be a dustbin of scraps of brilliant fabric, odd gems, worthless but fascinating curiosities, tinsel, quaint bits of carving, and a reasonable amount of healthy dirt. Shake the machine and it goes out of order; shake the dustbin and it adjusts itself beautifully to its new position."

ROBERTSON DAVIES, *TEMPEST-TOST*

The word "technocrat" can be misleading. In my experience, people tend to conjure up a bureaucrat; someone who works (sort of) for the government. But I have in mind a more precise definition; a technocrat is *someone who emphasizes the technical conceptions of a problem to the detriment of their social and human consequences.* Which translates to something like, *I understand that you may lose your house/job/car, but it says here in my rule book that I can't make exceptions.* Now, this person may work quickly or slowly, may be dedicated or lazy, highly intelligent, even brilliant, or just average. What counts is the attachment to rules, written or unwritten. The unwritten rules are otherwise known as conventional wisdom.

My group of Technocrats is superficially very diverse. Some are slow, even ponderous, in their thinking habits and mannerisms. Some are like hares; they run fast, talk fast, think fast and argue circles around the competition. They are tall and short and in between. They've had many different jobs in their lifetimes: engineers, consultants, accountants, managers of very different kinds of organizations. Some are exceedingly well-read, others not. They like to collect art — you're supposed to, you know.[1] Some smile and others don't, but when it gets down to business, none of them do. As one said to me, "I laugh as much as the next guy — at home. Work is for working." These men are not funny.

They are rigid. They possess *Truth*. They disdain all those whose reasoning processes are not up to scratch, all those whose logic is infected with, and corrupted by, passion. Colloquially we say, "He has a mind like a steel trap." You can get caught in it like a vise. It's cold, remorseless, even fatal.

Technocrats are difficult to get to know. One Craftsman who worked with them for years told me in frustration, "I don't know what makes them tick. I can't get a grip on them." Personally I've known some of these Technocrats for more than ten years, and I still can't get a grip on them, either. You have the sense of talking to a wall; you can try to crash through it, but on the other side you're in just another empty room. It makes you mad, increases your emotional response, and then they dismiss you for the very emotion they themselves have engendered! It's a vicious circle.

Following is the map of how they are seen by their friends and enemies, board members and peers. At the core: no-nonsense, intense, determined, uncompromising, fastidious, cerebral, hard-headed. To the south, where they look a little like Craftsmen, they are recognized as hardworking. To the extreme west, serious, analytical, methodical, detail-oriented, meticulous. Moving northward, distant, stiff. In the northeast, difficult. Turning southward, brilliant, insightful, energetic. You see, when you swing from extreme west to extreme east, you go from ponderous to quick. This is an illustration of the superficial differences that can seem to separate, say, Cam from David and that can mislead us radically. Brilliance and insight, for example, can and often do masquerade as vision.

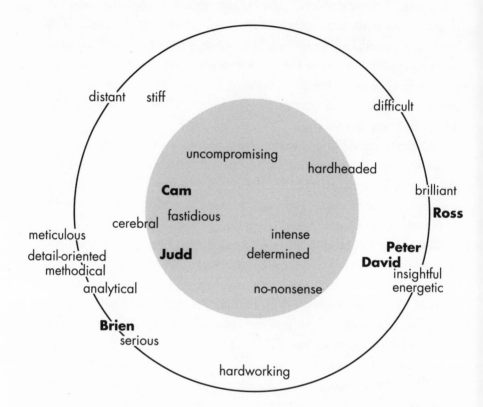

Analytical is good. Methodical is good. Serious can be good. Brilliant can be good. Insightful, were it coupled with honest and modest, would certainly be good. Almost any one of these qualifiers, taken individually or in pairs, is complimentary, even flattering. Taken together, we have a syndrome. The Technocrat. Let's look at our groups again: behaviour, thought processes and temperament.

B EHAVIOUR

He is methodical, fastidious, uncompromising, difficult, determined, energetic, hardworking. A member of one of the boards had this to say about a Technocrat:

> Very methodical, looked into opportunities very thoroughly. Stubborn. Big ego. Thinks a certain way and so should everyone else. Very arrogant. Well-organized. Brought out his notes from a meeting six months ago and asked what had been done since.

This was no casual observer. He had known this particular Technocrat for fifteen years. What he said to me in private, however, he had never dared even to imply in public. He knew from hard experience that he wouldn't be around very long if he didn't keep his thoughts to himself.

Methodical. Fastidious. The Oxford dictionary defines fastidious as "selecting carefully; choosing only what is good." He "looked into opportunities very thoroughly." Yes, but you say, isn't that simply prudent, wise? Then, I reply, how come no one ever calls him wise? No. This was not normal prudence. This was prudence pushed to the edge. This was crossing every "t" and dotting every "i." This was trying, desperately, to ensure against any error.

Uncompromising. Not uncompromising in the sense of, say, unswerving, uncompromising, loyalty in the pursuit of some moral principle, but in the sense of *stubborn, big ego*. Another board member remembers a particularly distasteful incident in a committee meeting with the same Technocrat:

> He sat right there and we all disagreed with him. Afterwards, he went into the full board meeting and reported exactly what he had argued with us — and lost — as though it was the view of the committee. It was like the committee meeting hadn't even taken place!

I was there too and this is exactly what happened. I felt like Alice in Wonderland. He was, to say the least, difficult and hardheaded. You know, to this day, I don't think he did this on purpose. He did it because he was hardheaded in the literal sense of the word "hard," in the sense of impermeable. It was as though everything we had said could not penetrate. Sort of like water off a duck's back. And he was very determined to have his way.

Yes, the Technocrat works hard and is energetic. But his working hard is not because he's passionately committed to a task, but because working hard is a *rule*: people are supposed to work hard. It is a measure of the worth of a man how many hours he puts in and how few vacations he takes. Life is a serious affair.

THOUGHT PROCESSES

The Technocrat is seen as meticulous, detail-oriented, analytical, insightful, brilliant. The first three tend rather naturally to go together. If you are meticulous, it means you examine the details of something. If you conduct an analysis of something, it means you look at its parts and their interrelationship; you break down, somewhat artificially, some phenomenon into its constituent parts. Which is what I am doing now — looking at various parts of the Technocrat character to try to understand how it works. But some things do not benefit from being broken down into parts; they lose their essence this way — an idea, a sunset, a poem. The German poet Goethe was furious when people asked him what his novel *Werther* was about; he felt he had struggled long and hard to fuse it into a meaningful whole and people were asking him to break it up again into meaningless parts:

> This made me very angry and I insulted a good many people. For me, in order to answer the question, I would have had to take my little book, over which I had brooded so long in order to fuse its various elements into a poetic oneness, and tear it to bits again and destroy its form.[2]

If you are detail-oriented you are likely to be analytical, to want to see the intricate workings of various parts. And when the various parts are all displayed before your eyes, you may be able to pick out some flaws. Then it will be said you are insightful: "Oh yes. I see now. I'd missed that detail. Now I understand. How *insightful* of you to have seen this." In the fifth century B.C., a celebrated Sophist was able to pick out several "flaws" in the first few lines of Homer's *Iliad* and was recognized, by everyone but Socrates, to have been very insightful.[3] But Socrates wasn't big on the Sophists, and Homer's "flawed" poem has lasted quite a while.

In the context of vision, let's look at Dali again, this time with technocratic eyes. The first thing to remember is that the overall design is given to the Technocrat — he doesn't dream it up himself; analysis can only follow creation. In the words of one of them:

> It's not the CEO's job to create the ideas; his job is to sift and measure ideas that come from somewhere or someone else.

Incidentally, this is almost word for word what Santayana told us: "Man's progress has a poetic phase in which he imagines the world and a scientific phase in which he sifts and tests what he imagines." So the Technocrat analyses the design, breaks it into parts. He discovers that the tree doesn't *belong* in the middle. He discovers that two of the buildings are dilapidated and should be condemned. He discovers that curves — and people — are inefficient and should give way to straight lines and uniform scale. There are no trees here. The drawing is not very "realistic." By the way, we no longer see the horizon. We are too fixed on the details to lift our eyes toward a distant and unknown future; indeed, there is no longer any road opening to the future.

If you get very, very good at all this analysis, you are apt to be called brilliant, as in, "That was a brilliant presentation." The original meaning of brilliant is something shiny, sparkling, like a diamond. Overlaying this are connotations of rigour and precision. The application of "brilliant" to human mentation was rare before the eighteenth century. Is this

U.K.
BANK

CAYMAN
BANK

U.S.
GENERAL
INSURANCE

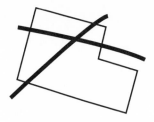

CAYMAN
INSURANCE

U.S.
LIFE
COMPANY

an accident, or does it coincide with the Enlightenment? Jefferson talked earlier about the strong "penetration" of Locke, Bacon and Newton; I think he meant that these men were powerfully analytic. In any event, all that glitters is not gold — or diamonds. But one thing is sure, diamonds are tough — we use them to drill through rock — and cold. Sometimes we call them rocks and sometimes ice. Let's look at temperament.

TEMPERAMENT

Serious, distant, stiff, intense, no-nonsense, cerebral. The Technocrat is cold. The room temperature drops three degrees when he enters. Everyone gets quiet and usually stops smiling. Serious looks get plastered on faces, like when kids are joking around and the third-grade teacher shows up. "All right. No nonsense, children. We're here to work, not to play." They're distant and stiff, and that's why we heard a Craftsman say earlier, "I can't get a grip on them. I don't know what makes them tick." And it's why, after many years, we know them no better than before.

There are thick walls around their emotions. In addition to our conscious thoughts, it's through our emotional contact that we get to know one another. Have you ever wanted to cozy up to "brilliant"? How about taking in a second-rate movie, just for relaxation? Do you invite "brilliant" along? Technocrats are so intense, seem to be under such rigid control, take things, and especially themselves, so seriously that grown adults begin to feel like foolish children around them. So that's why people see them as cerebral, which, according to Oxford, means "of the brain; intellectual [as opposed to emotional]." To some it may seem inappropriate that I have placed "cerebral" in the temperament category instead of in thought processes. But we all *think*. What is different with cerebral is that it excludes affect or emotion. It is just this exclusion that defines the word. In everyday usage, a cerebral person is someone who, paradoxically, telegraphs the emotion that emotion is unacceptable. Why?

INNER LIFE

In a word, defence. Affect, emotion, is at the core of character. If we are frightened, for example, we develop defences against fear: flight, fight, hide, deny, forget, whistle (you know, whistling in the dark). Depending on our endowments, our choice of defence and the situations we encounter, our character will be shaped; we will develop "characteristic" ways of behaving and thinking, "characteristic" ways of reacting to people, to events, to ideas, to the world. This is the essential reason why many psychiatric texts have in their titles "bio-psycho-socio," in that order. Now I'm not going to subject you to a treatise on why these men became they way they are. I know literally nothing about their genetic makeup, their relations with their mothers and fathers or anything else of a personal nature. But I am going to talk about the end result — the psycho and its relations with the socio.

Here is a typical MMPI profile of a Technocrat as interpreted by the clinical psychologist (remember, he did not know who this person was nor what I thought about him):

> This guy's very defensive, psychically well defended. Not admitting to anything serious. More sensitive than he would like to be perceived. Chronic worrier. Lots churning around inside that's never talked about. There's a flair of creativity but — this is the key — it's repressed and denied. Under stress, he's paranoid (can't trust anyone but himself) and will project blame unto others. He's isolated, angry, tense, cold, rigid, brilliant — like Eichmann.

There's that word "brilliant" again. Sure enough, in the group of fifteen men, this man had the second-highest rating on "brilliant." He also had far and away the highest rating on "distant" and "stiff"; the second-highest on "uncompromising" and "difficult"; zero on people-oriented, amiable, exciting, warm, generous, easygoing, realistic, open-minded. Appearances — the adjectives — reflect the inner world. Two technocratic peers said he was "inspiring"; what you see depends on where you sit. They "identified" with him.[4]

Let's look a little more closely at the profile to try to understand what's going on. "Very defensive, psychically well defended"; when we use the word "defensive," what does it mean? Take the following incident:

> "Did you spill the milk?"
>
> "Yes, but there was so much clutter on the countertop I couldn't help it, and furthermore I've asked you a thousand times not to put the toaster next to the fridge. So it's not my fault."
>
> "Don't get *defensive*. I only meant did *you* spill the milk or did Billy. I'm trying to teach him to clean up his own messes."
>
> "Oh."

This man is "psychically well defended" against criticism. He assumes that he will be blamed (a bit paranoid), and he develops a host of arguments to defend against this anticipated blame; one of them is to find a way to blame someone else. Sometimes, as in this incident, the blame he anticipates is not forthcoming; his judgement is bad. He "imagines" it. He "projects" the fault onto others because he cannot bear the thought that he is less than perfect. Less than perfect is dangerous, unacceptable. He's very hard on himself and thus very hard on others. In the organizational context, one Craftsman said of him, "His attitude was always 'I found the mistake and I fired the son of a bitch.' It's never his fault." There's an element of narcissism in this too; not narcissism in the popular sense of egotistical, but in the clinical sense of "enraged by criticism."[5] Criticism, explicit or implicit, real or imagined, would tarnish the perfect image he needs to maintain for others, but especially for himself.

"Lots churning around inside." Lots of emotions — anger, joy, sadness — but they're "repressed and denied." The psychologist is using technical language, but what do "repressed" and "denied" mean to us? Repressed — consciously eliminated from thought. Denied — unconsciously eliminated from thought, the simplest example being something like, "You were supposed to go to the dentist." "I forgot." These people "forget" their lost emotions. The elevation of certain scales in the profile "seems to reflect the aggressive or hostile feelings and impulses that are present to a significant degree, while the scale-three height in turn shows that repressive and suppressive controls are even stronger than the impulse. . . . Although inhibited and moderate, [they] episodically express their aggressive feelings directly and intensely."[6] A Craftsman would tell me of one Technocrat, "If you disagree with him, he explodes on contact." But most of the time they are the picture of serenity. They seem imperturbable. Everything is under control. Just follow the plan and the orders, and everything will be all right.

Following orders is important. One of the highlights of the personality disorder called the "compulsive personality" is that interpersonal relations are organized around dominance and submission. As a subordinate he may seem agreeable, submissive, even obsequious. Once in power, however, he will brook no opposition and will evidence an unreasonable insistence that others submit to exactly his way of doing things; he will show an unreasonable reluctance to allow others to do things because of the conviction they will not do them correctly.[7] But this is intimately related both to the paranoid tinge and to the fear of failure. The script reads something like, "If I'm in absolute control and I'm perfect, then nothing can go wrong. I must make these others submit to my way of doing things. It's for their own good." For the most part, I think, the Technocrat usually believes that what he does is for the benefit of everyone. He thinks his superior intelligence grants him good judgement. To him, the others are wayward children. This is exactly how Frederick Winslow Taylor, the father of Scientific Management and a notorious compulsive, talked about "the workers." He wanted to "help" them by so breaking their work down to the minutest of details, so that conflict and doubt and confusion and disorder would all be eliminated. "Workmen" would make a lot of money, employers would make lots of profit and everyone would be happy — an industrial utopia. The "facts" spoke for themselves. His system was foolproof — with the minor exception that workers hated it and didn't want to "submit" even "for their own good." And the odd thing is, this guy Taylor, who wanted desperately to have peace and calm, created nothing but conflict around him and regularly "exploded on contact."[8]

Taylor's breaking work down to the minutest of details also typifies the compulsive personality: preoccupation with details, rules, lists, order, systems, organization or schedules to the extent that the major point of the activity is lost. One Craftsman would say of the Technocrats:

> I don't know. Their strategy was very murky. They seemed to be fascinated by tinkering with the thing. You know, systems, structures.

They're big on facts. They're big on organizational charts. Very big on systems and structures and rules. This orientation toward details and systems often means that these men develop technical virtuosity. They succeed based upon it. Of course it has a price. What distinguishes a personality disorder from a neurosis is that the person himself does not suffer — he thinks he's just fine — but the people around him do. Technocrats miss the "tone" of social situations because they are too concentrated on the details and facts. Depth psychologist David Shapiro describes the compulsive character (emphasis is mine):

> These people seem unable to allow their attention simply to wander or passively permit it to be captured. Thus, they rarely get hunches, and they are rarely struck or surprised by anything. It is not that they don't look or listen, but that they are *looking and listening too hard* for something else. For example, these people may listen to a recording with the keenest interest in, and attention to, the quality of the equipment, the technical features of the record, and the like, but meanwhile hardly hear, let alone are captured by, the music. In general, the obsessive-compulsive person will have some sharply-defined interest

and stick to it; he will go after and get the facts — and will get them straight — but he will often miss those aspects of the situation that give it its flavour or impact. Thus, these people often seem insensitive to the "*tone*" of social situations. In fact — such is the human capacity to make a virtue of necessity — they often refer with pride to their single-mindedness or imperturbability.[9]

They don't know that their orientation toward the facts is part of their character. They lack personal insight and think themselves reasonable, realistic and sensible. This lack of personal insight is the other thing that comes out very strongly in the MMPI results for the Technocrats. The MMPI is a tricky test. It contains all sorts of traps. It has "validity indicators" based on some questions to which no one should answer "false." For example, my Technocrats answered "false" to the statement "I get angry sometimes," or to the statement "At times I feel like swearing." Several of the Technocrat profiles were close to invalidation for these kinds of responses. In general, the MMPI tells us:

> Valid elevations in the high to markedly elevated ranges are most likely to be generated by subjects who are honestly describing themselves as they see themselves. They tend, therefore, to be overly conventional, socially-conforming and prosaic. Some of the descriptions actually correspond to their habitual patterns of behaviour while other features of their test answers reflect their poor insight and limited self-knowledge.

They really do not see themselves. Thus, while they think themselves realistic, no one else (except maybe another Technocrat) does. And they see themselves as honest, but no one else does. In an interview with a Craftsman, I noticed that he had failed to mark "honest" for any of the Technocrats. I asked him why. He replied, reluctantly, "I suppose they're honest, but they're certainly not straightforward." It's hard to be honest with others if you don't know yourself, and this absence of authenticity makes itself felt. We will see this more clearly later.

One of the best ways to deny your feelings, and it's the preferred strategy of Technocrats, is to cut your feelings off from the thoughts that go with them. Professionals call this "isolation." It shows up in typical fashion in this Technocrat's description:

> Oh, him, he's a great guy. I like him. We still have lunch together. He just couldn't do the job, that's all. He understood this. It was nothing personal. Just business.

You see, there is no emotion, no affect here. Just thought. Night follows day. Facts are facts. No hard feelings. Needless to say, the "great guy" he was talking about despises him. A very close cousin of "isolation" is "intellectualization," which "represents an attempt to avoid objectionable impulses or affects by escaping from the world of emotions into a world of intellectual concepts and words."[10] That's why the Technocrat sometimes sounds like a talking machine. He has lots of high-blown theory that bears little relation to his actions. One Craftsman had this to say about one of them:

> He used to quote Drucker to us all the time, saying that you could have centralization or decentralization but nothing in between. So he said he was in favour of decentralization. But, of course, he was doing just the opposite.

He always justified, rationalized, "intellectualized" his actions, usually by relying on some "expert" (read — a guy from out of town).

An Artist said of another Technocrat:

> Oh, sure. He was always talking about decentralization, but every single move he made was centralizing. Everybody knew it. It was just for the parade.

Everyone thought the Technocrats were habitual liars (which is why no one thought they were honest), but I'm not so sure they were consciously duplicitous. My impression is that Technocrats sincerely believe their conventional ideas — if Drucker says it, it must be right.

They simply can't help themselves. They are strangers to themselves as much as they are to others. Their need to be in control, to dominate, to prevent mistakes, automatically causes them to act in a way that removes authority from everyone else. As we will see later, they intellectualize this process with the fanciest of reasoning.

So. With their emotions securely buttoned-up, except for rare explosions, and with grand intellectual schemes to impose, they come across as cold, rigid and brilliant. Others mistrust them because underneath their protestations of kindness, underneath their mouthing of the importance of teamwork, lurks the uncompromising hostility and self-righteousness that everyone dreads — "It's my way or the highway." Fearing the unknown and the uncontrollable, logic, science, rational analysis become their passwords, because these things promise to control and to tame an otherwise frightening and uncertain future. Under stress, they project their forgotten emotions onto others, calling them emotional, impulsive. They blame others for the errors an uncertain world inevitably gives rise to. Once he has ordered his world, the Technocrat is stubborn about changing his view. He is conservative because change is deeply menacing to him. This is part of his character.

The Technocrat Character

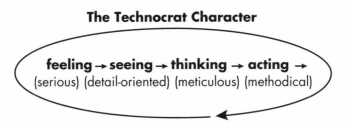

feeling → seeing → thinking → acting →
(serious) (detail-oriented) (meticulous) (methodical)

Can you teach someone who is serious, detail-oriented, meticulous and methodical to be imaginative, wise, entrepreneurial or funny? If so, you're a better teacher than I.

So far, I have given you the three characters in relatively splendid isolation. In the next chapter, we're going to see them all together. In the chapter after that, you'll see them interacting on the organizational stage.

Scientific statements are, as people say now, far more easily "cashed". But the poet might of course reply that it always will be easier to cash a cheque for 30 shillings than one for 1000 pounds, that the Scientific statements are cheques, in one sense, for very small amounts, giving us, out of the teeming complexity of every concrete reality, only the "common measurable features". Such information as Poetic language has to give can be received only if you are ready to meet it half way. It is no good holding a dialectical pistol to the poet's head and demanding how the deuce a river could have hair, or thought be green, or a woman a red rose. . . . If he had anything to tell you, you will never get it by behaving in that way. You must begin by trusting him. Only by doing so will you find out whether he is trustworthy or not. *Credo ut intelligam.* . . .

C. S. LEWIS, *CHRISTIAN REFLECTIONS*

Given what you know now, do you think the Technocrat could trust the Artist long enough to find out whether or not he is trustworthy? Not on your life. Do you think he would try "holding a dialectical pistol" to the Artist's head? Try to force him to define the undefinable? You're right. Well, that's just a beginning. What we're going to do now is put those little circles I gave you in the preceding chapters into perspective. The circles, the characters, exist in relation to one another and not in the artificial, analytical isolation in which I first presented them.

On the following page you'll see the whole map. I have superimposed the circles on it so you can follow the cast of characters. We

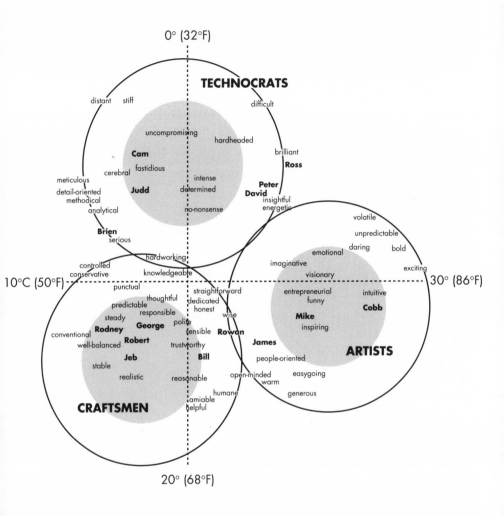

talked first about the Artists. Here they are again, next to their friends, the Craftsmen, and literally opposite their enemies. Look at Cobb. You might think that he is most different from Brien, Brien being at the opposite end of the spectrum. But here's the trick: he's almost on the same level as Brien on the horizontal plane; he shares something with Brien. The person Cobb is most unlike is Cam. Cam is in the northwest, Cobb in the southeast. Both dimensions count. Got it? This is how we're going to proceed.

There are multiple levels of interpretation of this graph, so I hope you'll be patient. First, it can be read like an organizational thermometer. Start in the extreme east and it's very hot, about 30°C — exciting. The organizational melody is like a concerto with one key guy — Cobb, Mike or James, take your pick — leading it. When you're inside the organization, everyone is working diligently and everyone seems happy. Some are breathing hard because things are really hopping. A dozen crucial projects are under way. They're attacking on all fronts.

As you move southward, the temperature gets milder, more temperate, around 25°C. You pass from hot to warm. From Cobb to James, you're moving from the Artist territory into the Craftsman territory. In the fancy arithmetic I mentioned earlier (also see Technical Appendix), James "loads" mainly on the Artist, but partially on the Craftsman. Moving due west, you pass through Bill and Rowan who have some artistic leanings but are basically Craftsmen. In the heart of the Craftsman profile we pass from warm into neutral territory. It's now a very comfortable 20°C, and everyone goes about his business at a straightforward, relatively calm pace. Relations are cordial but not effusive. There are lots of smiles but little uproarious laughter.

As we round the cape and start to move northward again, past Rodney and reaching up to Brien, there's a distinct chill in the air. Let's say the workplace is dull; nobody's particularly enthusiastic but neither are they comatose. We're in *serious* territory. Pushing past Brien up to Judd and Cam, this is Chicago in January. Stiff, distant, uncompromising, cold. Brrr. Inside the organization, it's like a morgue. No one talks about anything except business. Chatting is frivolous. The corridors are silent. All the office doors are closed and you just know there is very, very serious work indeed under way behind those closed doors. There are an equal number of projects here as there are in the artistic organization, but they all have to do with financing, with systems, with internal and external audits.

As you round the top and start to move toward the territory of David and Peter and especially Ross, it starts to get hot again, but it's the heat of a blast furnace and not of a tropical sun. That's not a very kind image, you say. Well, it's not meant to be. I'll tell you why, because this moves us to the next level of interpretation.

It's this business about the horizontal and the vertical axes and their relationships. The heat of the Artists is tempered by their affinities with the Craftsmen. Cobb, Mike and James are all *below* the horizontal axis. Ross, on the other hand, is well *above* it. All the people up north are radically non-Craftsman. That is, they are *not* seen to be, among other things, honest, trustworthy, amiable, easygoing or generous. In fact, they are only hot in the sense of intense, demanding. They are impatient and they often explode on contact. The more positioned to the right of the vertical axis, the more emotional, but the emotions up north are not pretty ones. In fact, they can be downright ugly. Thus, when people tell me that the secret to great leadership is authenticity and letting out what's inside, being spontaneous and all that, I get nervous. I don't particularly want these guys to be spontaneous. I would just as soon they kept their emotions to themselves — or confided them to a therapist. Their repression is good — for the rest of us.

So let's get back to Brien. Brien does not usually explode on contact. But he, and all those positioned in the west — Rodney, Brien, Judd and Cam — are radically non-Artist. That is, they are radically *not* intuitive, inspiring, entrepreneurial or funny. They are instead controlled, conservative, methodical and cerebral. If we look at

Rodney, for example, he's a long way from Cobb but an almost equal distance from Cam, even though he's methodical like Cam. You would think he wouldn't get along with either of them. Wrong. He gets along very well with Cobb. Let's try to understand why.

Imagine you are sitting down in the southeast corner close to James. When you look diagonally across the map you see your opposite. You see cold, cerebral. You see Cam and Judd. Do you hate them? Okay, now move across and sit in Cam and Judd's shoes and look back at James — intuitive, funny, inspiring. Are you inspired? Do you think he's funny? Think carefully before you answer. Remember, you are now stiff, methodical and serious. There's one clue, one key word here that makes all the difference in the world. Their reactions to each other, the Artist and the Technocrat, are *a*symmetrical. The Technocrat despises the Artist. The Artist tolerates, even appreciates, the Technocrat; as we will see later, one Artist will give a Technocrat total control over his organization. The key word is "open-minded," with a minor in "generous."

When the Artist looks at the Technocrat he doesn't hate him. He sees "brilliant." He sees "methodical." He sees his qualities and his virtues. He finds the Technocrat sort of stiff, but he's tolerant of it. He wants the "brilliant," for he wants to be challenged. He doesn't like yes-men. He wants to be stimulated. His mind is open. And he's a bit insecure about his own skills. He has doubts. His way of protecting himself is to have very strong people around him. People who have the courage to tell him when he's going off the rails. That's one of the many reasons he values the Craftsman, for the Craftsman is direct, frank.

But when the Technocrat looks at the Artist, he is not open-minded. He sees only faults. Here's what one Technocrat says:

> He was Startrecky. He produced a hundred new ideas, but only one of them would be useful. It's terribly inefficient and ineffective. The people underneath get *frustrated*. It's awe-inspiring but eventually demotivating. Our world cannot do without them, but our organizations sure can.

Another adds:

> We had to protect the organization from him. *He drove people crazy with his ideas.* No one knew what he should be working on at any one time. Everyone was running around in all directions.

And still another:

> He simply was not a manager. He was over his head. He was an adviser. He was volatile, unpredictable, imaginative, visionary. A nice guy. Very amiable. The kind of guy you might seek ideas from but not the guy to run something. *He didn't know how to work.*

This is what happens when "serious" looks at "funny." It sees red. "He didn't know how to work." Translation: he was not serious; he took vacations. "He drove people crazy." Translation: he drove *me* crazy. "The people underneath get frustrated." Translation: *I* got frustrated. Others in these organizations were much more apt to tell me things like, "You work for a guy like him only once in your life." That was said with deep admiration. As for the guy who "didn't know how to work," a senior member of his board told me, "He was very well mannered and considerate. He fired people, but he did it nicely (if firing can ever be nice). He was *hardworking* and *very dedicated*." I didn't hear any frustration except from the Technocrats. The Craftsmen weren't frustrated at all.

On the contrary, the Craftsman respects the Artist. Oh, he thinks he sometimes goes too far and too fast, but he thinks Artists are indispensable; one told me, "The analytic boys are a dime a dozen, but you can't buy dreams." Yet the Craftsman, normally open-minded, shuts down when it comes to Technocrats. He's the one who gets intransigent, stubborn. This is essentially because the Craftsman has his feet most firmly planted on the ground; he doesn't mind being lifted off occasionally by the Artist, by a dream, but he resists with all his might getting carried away by a theory. He finds the Technocrat, and his managerial theories, his maxims, totally unrealistic. This is what

Craftsmen say about Technocrats:

> They seemed to think that you could grow and expand and not have an impact on the bottom line. But any schoolboy knows better. They're like the little old lady who wants capital gains and income. Totally *unrealistic*.

> You can't correct a problem unless you see it exists. It's like me. I look in the mirror and I see a young fullback, not a balding, middle-aged man with his chest on his belly. You have to see *reality* to change it.

> Why can't they *see* it, they're brilliant? I guess if, with all their brilliance they can *rationalize* it all away, we all rationalize.

> They didn't really understand our situation . . . *too distant from the coalface* to understand how the business works.

"Too distant from the coalface," that is, too theoretical, impractical, not experienced enough to know the difference between a good idea and a bad one, a new idea and an old one dressed up in a pretty new skirt. The Craftsman values experience, hands-on experience. He doesn't believe that you can get to know something only by reading about it. You have to be there. That's why he thinks the Technocrat makes a good consultant but a lousy manager, and even if he's his boss, he says so.

The Technocrat, on the other hand, doesn't value experience. For him, experience equals old-fashioned. He values "brain power." Here's a taste of technocratic opinions about Craftsmen:

> He can be a useful number-two man. He can be counted on to keep the ship afloat in stable waters. Once the direction is set [read, by us], he can keep it running for a while. But after a time, the disease sets in. Inefficiencies. And when the waters get troubled, when the marketplace is fluid, he's hopeless . . . he doesn't have the *brain power*.

> We have to put some *talent* in there. He's just not *strong* enough.

I have a feeling that he's over his *head*. Not really up to general management. Really a second-level kind of guy.

It's not that he's stubborn. He's just too *stupid* to follow the line of reasoning.

They're *incompetent*.

Hear the disdain, the condescension? Some of these "incompetent" Craftsmen had been running businesses while many of the Technocrats were still in high school. Now, experience is not always profitable. Some people *are* old-fashioned and closed-minded. But every one of them? Don't forget that these Craftsmen are seen to be open-minded by the vast majority of their colleagues. They resist change all right, but only when the change is for them unrealistic.

The irony is of course that the Technocrats see themselves as realistic, sensible and reasonable, but they are all alone. They also see themselves generally as entrepreneurial, intuitive and imaginative, but they are all alone. One described another to me as an entrepreneur. Because he was the only one to say so, I was curious about his definition of entrepreneur, so I asked him to elaborate. "An entrepreneur," he said, "is someone who is stingy, someone who treats the corporation's money as if it was his own." That was the most bizarre definition of "entrepreneur" I had ever heard. No wonder, then, that another Technocrat told me:

James, Cobb and Rowan, they were all dreamers not entrepreneurs. They're what I call advisers. Now we have builders. They're conservative of course, but if you're not conservative you'll lose everything.

This takes us back to the problem of personal insight. Technocrats lack insight into their own characters and into others'. I very nearly burst out laughing when the coldest, most rigid of them said of another, "Him. Oh, he's a very cold man. Frigid. Very distant." The person he was talking about was the life of the party next to him.

Even within the group of Technocrats, there are problems. One of them referred to his colleagues as "a bunch of amateurs." Others felt that some of their peers, their rivals for power, were not really "professional" [read, technical] enough. Of course, if you possess *Truth* and you *need* to impose *your* truth, everyone is a dangerous rival. You have to find some way to undermine the other's credibility. Those who were outwardly calm and collected were suspicious of anyone who was more emotional; they said things like, "He'll have to be watched and controlled," or, "He can fly off in all directions." They are really deeply suspicious of "emotional." In fact, they use it as the worst kind of insult. Of course, anyone who needs desperately to be in control will have a hard time working in the traces of a team no matter what its composition.

So, inside the organization, behind the scenes, we hear a cacophony of people shouting insults at one another: "emotional," "unrealistic," "dreamer," "theoretician," "incompetent," "old-fashioned." They think they are arguing about substance, when in fact they are arguing about character. Each sees the organizational landscape differently. Each interprets it differently. The same "facts" have different meanings. One is buoyantly optimistic and occasionally discouraged. One is moderately optimistic. One is deeply pessimistic, even phobic. Whose interpretation will carry the day?

The Technocrat's. Let's watch how he steals the scene.

II

The Play

Five   The Dreams of the Playwright

There is, however, no basic vocabulary of lines and colours, or ele-
mental tonal structures, or poetic phrases, with conventional emo-
tive meanings from which complex expressive forms, i.e., works of
art, can be composed by rules of manipulation. . . . It is easy
enough to produce standard cadences, manufacture hymn tunes
according to familiar models and some experiential knowledge of
standard alternative resolutions, etc.; but such products are at best
mediocre. . . . The analysis of spirited, noble or moving work is
always retrospective. . . .

S. K. LANGER, *MIND: AN ESSAY ON HUMAN FEELING*[1]

We have seen that there have been three Ideal Types of leaders
involved in the life of the organization. The Artist appears volatile and
imaginative, corresponding to an inner life that is cyclothymic (up and
down) and autistic (his capacity, or indeed his need, to dream).

The Technocrat, on the other hand, is seen to be meticulous,
cerebral and, often, brilliant, as well as difficult, uncompromising and
emotionally cold. These are the outward manifestations of inner psy-
chic processes: fear of the unconscious and the emotions, which causes a generalized suppression of all emotion, along with a disdain for it
in others. His fears also engender an unreasonable attachment to the
security afforded by conventional wisdom: If everybody thinks it's
true, it must be. His need to intellectualize, coupled with above-average intelligence, makes him a powerful analyst and a dangerous foe.

The Craftsman is not simply midway between the two, a residual category like "all others." He is honest and dedicated, loyal and straightforward. He is intelligent, forceful in defence of his values, with an appreciation of hands-on experience that sets him apart from his fellows. Psychically, he is more than Everyman; he has above-average drive, otherwise he would not have sought positions of power. He is polite but not a pushover; he refuses to hide his values in order to survive.

I'm sure you can already imagine how these three characters would interact on the organizational stage. This chapter retells their story from the far-from-dispassionate point of view of the actors themselves. The names and places are fictitious, but the events are not.

THE EARLY YEARS

Our story opens in Small City, U.K., in the 1960s. The aging chairman of the board of a forty-year-old, medium-size, general insurance company — ABC Company — is preparing to retire. He does not have confidence in the ability of any of his employees to take over the managerial reins. Recently he has come into contact with James, the young owner of a small rival company, and was very favourably impressed with the man's style. Self-taught, James seemed to have a sophistication beyond his years and to have established a reputation as both scrupulously honest and farsighted. The chairman courts him. The younger man is not anxious to give up his entrepreneurial freedom. Finally, after a great deal of soul-searching, and with the prospect of much wider horizons before him, he accepts. Within a year, James is firmly in control. Within eighteen months he makes his first acquisition. For the next ten years, the aging chairman cannot catch his breath. He never regrets his decision.

In 1965 ABC Company had a small but important hold on its regional market. A local "favourite son," it benefitted from its reputation for strengthening the local economy (indeed that was its *raison d'être*);

"home rule" sentiment was running high. Whereas previous management had been content to tap this local sentiment, James felt that more could be done; the whole of the country could benefit from the success of a local firm. However, at normal growth rates, ABC Company's relatively small scale gave the absolute growth advantage to its foreign-owned competitors. "If we and company X had both grown at the same rate per year," James figured, "then they would have added two hundred million sterling to assets while we added only ten. They would have got farther and farther ahead of us. That's why we had to acquire."

With a limited capital base, a property-and-casualty company is restricted in its capacity to make large acquisitions. James, now the chairman, decided to solve his dilemma in two ways. During the course of the first acquisition, a troubled local insurer, he had come into contact with the large European Financial Group (EFC), which had held a controlling interest in that firm. James had negotiated a sweetheart deal with EFC, which brought that company both peace of mind and steady dividends on its remaining minority interest. James's personal charm and astute negotiating skills — not taking advantage of EFC's momentary weakness — had earned him permanent, and wealthy, friends. He created a "strategic alliance" *twenty years before* academics started talking about such things. He was to use this alliance repeatedly over the next decade, and his formula for controlling a target with less than fifty percent of the stock was to allow him to leverage ABC Company's limited assets far beyond their paper worth.

The second axis of his strategy was to buy a life insurance company. Because life insurance contracts and liabilities are very long-term compared with general insurance, a life company builds up enormous assets. Controlling those assets gave James a pool of capital much more interesting to play with, and play he did. He bought a real estate company. Taking over a holding company in order to get his hands on its insurance assets, he acquired shares in a small bank and a building society. Believing that the future belongs to those who see it coming, he bought "modern communication" companies, companies that might just end up providing the best way to sell insurance. (And this was *twenty-five years before* anyone started talking about the Electronic Highway.) While his competitors sat smugly and safely behind the walls of their sectors — banking, general insurance, brokerage, life insurance — he broke out of the "industry recipe" and out of the borders of the financial sector as a whole (*twenty years before* anyone else). Personally indefatigable, with a restless, effervescent energy, he was never content to rest on his laurels. In his home country, he was third in general insurance, sixth in life; there was much to do.

Well-known by then, he was in the network — a man on the rise — and because he had a reputation for moving decisively when opportunity presented itself, many prospective deals were brought to his attention. In 1976 he was on an airplane with an acquaintance whom he knew to be dissatisfied with the performance of his British life company. He whispered in his ear that if ever this gentleman wished to sell, he would be interested. The call came shortly thereafter. With some fancy legal footwork, and the assistance and participation of the ever-present EFC, he managed to swallow the London-based life company, which was many times his size. Jubilation was the order of the day. Not only did he now have an important presence in a major world financial centre, but the life company had subsidiaries in Hong Kong, Canada and the United States. In one sure move, he catapulted the previously obscure ABC Company onto the world stage. To the outside world, it looked opportunistic; to him, it was all part of the design.

The following year saw him take over another London holding company, which allowed him to solidify his position in general insurance and pick up more shares in the banking and building society. In the process, he got more real estate for his real estate development company and a woollen mill. A decentralist by nature, he gave free rein to the local management in Canada and the United States, and assets began to climb there, as well. Finally, by the end of the first five-year period, he controlled the bank and was able to appoint his own man. It was now 1980. He'd been in power for fifteen years. For him the time seemed short.

His empire was big. He couldn't run it all. At the time of the British life company acquisition, he'd felt it necessary to hire a very senior man to oversee it, someone with more life insurance knowledge than he had. And he had to put someone in the bank. He continued to watch over general insurance, considering himself very ably seconded by an operating executive he had picked up and promoted during an earlier acquisition. The other disparate pieces were also his responsibility. Thus, by the end of the decade, the organizational structure and the people in it looked like the following chart. James was, of course, an Artist. Running the life company was a Technocrat and its U.S. and Canadian subsidiaries were run by an Artist and a Craftsman. There was a Craftsman at the bank, another one in general insurance, and a third with miscellaneous responsibilities.

Structure 1980

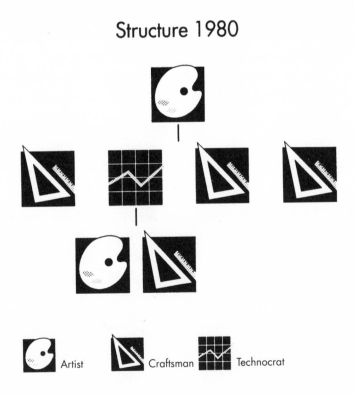

Artist   Craftsman   Technocrat

The Man, the Organizational Climate, the Strategy

What kind of man was this who was able to build an empire with few resources and in defiance of the conventional wisdom of the day when bankers and insurance executives had the reputation of being, at best, stuffy? Tall, strong and handsome, with the bearing of the Scottish king after whom he was named, James easily conquered all those he met. A board member told me:

> When he walked into that London boardroom for the first time after the takeover, everyone was on guard. Suspicious of the "upstart," these men expected the worst. They expected him to be both mediocre and arrogant.

By the end of the day, he had allayed both fears. He conceded that the Londoners knew more about their business than he did. He reassured them that he wouldn't interfere. He shook hands all around. He wined and dined and toasted their collective futures. He left having won them all over. What kind of magic did he have?

First of all, he had the magic of the Artist. Remember what one of his longtime associates, a woman, said of him?

> I was always astonished and puzzled by his capacity to sense the waves of the future before anyone else. Sometimes I thought of it as feminine intuition; the French call it *pif*, the nose for it. Like some kind of sixth sense.

He was always talking in images and metaphors about where ABC Company would be in twenty years — although he never put it on paper. As well, he had a prodigious memory. During heated negotiations, he didn't need to refer to financial crib sheets. He remembered all the numbers. The sentiments about him were almost universal: imaginative, intuitive, visionary. A one hundred percent score on energetic and entrepreneurial. These qualities made him an inspiring leader, a leader who gave people a sense of going somewhere and of participating in something important. He had a real gift, but this gift

92

alone can sometimes wear thin, and as important as these qualities were, it was perhaps his other side that kept people close, loyal and dedicated.

His other side was craft. Everyone, even his enemies, describe him as people-oriented, wise, honest; nine out of ten, as humane, amiable, warm. If you remember our map of the players, you see James positioned halfway between the Artists and the Craftsmen. And although he is a polar opposite of the Technocrat — appearing in the southeast opposite the Technocrats' northwest quadrant — his craft virtue of open-mindedness made him tolerant of other personal styles. He could work well with Artists, Craftsmen and Technocrats. He admired the Technocrat's skills. Self-taught himself, he had a tendency to be in awe of the formally trained. He scored zero on distant, stiff, cerebral, difficult and uncompromising. Unfortunately, for him and his organization, he also scored zero on meticulous and detail-oriented, and far too high on emotional.

The pure Technocrat, lacking the Artist/Craftsman's open-mindedness, found him beneath respect. James's vague images of a distant future struck the Technocrat as ridiculous, even foolish. James's passion, his dedication to social, economic and organizational causes, made him appear sentimental. His decisiveness and impulsiveness were anathema to someone who felt that management was a very serious affair, something that necessitated knowing exactly where one stood, having all the facts documented and the strategy clear. One told me with scorn in his voice: "Woollen mills, TV escapades. He didn't know what he was doing. It all had to be cleaned up. Put into order."

James talked in metaphors and what an admirer called images, a Technocrat detractor called riddles, which sometimes made no sense even after they were "decoded." This is always the Artist's cross to bear; his visions are often inarticulate. Remember James's version of the Dali painting in Chapter One? He was accused of not knowing what he was doing because the design was in his head and not a plan on paper. James says, in his own defence, "They accused me of diversifying, but I wasn't diversifying. These things were all related; they just didn't know it." But, I asked, what about the woollen mills and the other bits and pieces? "I wasn't interested in any of that stuff; I wanted the underlying assets. The other stuff was all sold at a profit."

If this lack of clarity was not enough to tarnish his reputation, his emotions were. One Technocrat said, "He's incapable of making a *logical* decision; he's too emotional; he cares about where head office is located; he doesn't understand that it's just a building; it's necessary to move. It makes economic sense." (The Technocrats wanted to move the head office from Small City to London; James insisted he had a moral commitment to stay. The Technocrats would eventually win.) Another added, "He was incapable of firing anyone. He was too close to his people. He always lets his *feelings* interfere with his judgement."

This was his Achilles' heel. It would prove crippling.

For the moment, however, he was still firmly in charge. His messages to shareholders in annual reports spoke to his central preoccupations: growth, the creation and maintenance of a corporate culture that enlists the creative outpouring of its employees, social progress for Small City and for his country. Poems introduced the message. In one, he almost apologized for having to report on earnings:

> Even though we don't believe an institution like ours should be judged strictly on the basis of the judicious and efficient use of resources, nevertheless, once a year we have to tally up. . . . Enough for numbers. . . ."

He very quickly went on to quote Saint-Exupéry on the importance of being larger than ourselves, carrying within us the hopes and dreams and well-being of others (*twenty years before* anyone talked about empowerment). Speaking of the corporation's reason for being, he talked about friendship and love:

Man reacts instinctively to the pressures of material need and the desire to live in friendship and love. It seems to us that to respond to these twin needs gives our institution a worthy reason for being.

To the Artist, the organization must root itself in moral imperatives to justify its existence.

James was not afraid of the future; with respect to its dangers, he wrote:

Our era demands much but promises even more! Even though we may feel a certain vertigo in front of the dangers, we can also taste — even exult in— the joys of knowing, creating, living.

Often philosophical, he dared to write publicly that aggression, animosity, even hatred are nothing but "an unconscious cry, an urgent appeal for more love." As though to underscore his point, he blanketed the cover of the annual report with hundreds of names of his employees. Harvard didn't tell him to do this. He did it instinctively. Finally, amidst all this talk of harmony and understanding, was always the note on growth. "An enterprise," he wrote, "must always be judged by its investment in the future and by the *ingenuity* with which it acts as a *pioneer*." As Polanyi told us earlier, "The explorer's fumbling progress is a much finer achievement than the well-briefed traveller's journey." And this was not "growth for growth's sake," but growth in order to accomplish great things for his country, for its citizens. Sentimental? Some thought so. In any event, as the next period opened, both he and the company he led were in full flight.

Six The Harsh Realities of the Stage

Blow, blow, thou winter wind,
Thou art not so unkind
As man's ingratitude:
Thy tooth is not so keen,
Because thou art not seen,
Although thy breath be rude.

SHAKESPEARE, *AS YOU LIKE IT*

The first two years of the 1980s were marked by the consolidation of the bank and another major acquisition in general insurance. Already, corporate assets were more than two billion sterling. James had been very busy. But another preoccupation began to weigh on his mind. Although still very vigorous (he still is at seventy-five!), he was in his mid-sixties and felt he must plan for succession. Long walks and long talks with his wife were the order of the day. Never arrogant, he told himself, "Sometimes a man can stay too long in an organization; it needs fresh air, a new approach." Anxious to provide ABC Company a secure future, he had doubts about his own continuing vision; he'd been taught, falsely, that vision is a characteristic only of the young. In his mind, there was only one man for the job, only one man with the breadth and the knowledge to understand all the pieces of the puzzle that had become his empire. This man had been with him since a major acquisition in the 1970s. He had the confidence of the board and he was all that James felt that he himself was not: brilliant, trained, solid, serious. In 1981 he invited Cam to accept the post of managing director. James would stay on as chairman. The offer was accepted.

To free both of them for other responsibilities necessitated hiring senior men for the two largest operating divisions. James and Cam together interviewed the candidates and jointly agreed upon two men. The Artist, James, continued in the chair and, effectively, remained very influential, with his power base rooted in the shareholders and EFC. A Technocrat, Cam, became the number-two man, and as fate would have it, the recruits turned out to be a Technocrat, Judd, and an Artist, Cobb.

As the number-two man, Cam had already become more and more influential. James allowed himself to be persuaded to sell off the "bits and pieces," which according to Cameron, "made no sense." James's dream of distributing financial services through electronic means had not come to fruition soon enough. According to Cam, it had been a pipedream (time and the Electronic Highway will tell). The communications interests were sold off. In fact, anything that was not, strictly speaking, financial services was sold off. Two new sectors were added by acquisition: investment banking and investment advisory companies as, by now, the whole world had begun to talk of the "collapse of the four pillars": banking, trust, insurance and brokerage. It had become the new "industry recipe" to be involved in all four and, where regulation permitted, to engage in cross-selling and marketing. *Synergy* became the new watchword.

Meanwhile, the two new men — Cobb and Judd — were settling into harness, and already things were beginning to heat up in the largest sector. Cobb, the Artist in charge there, seconded by Rowan, a Craftsman with entrepreneurial tendencies in the United States, and by another Artist, Mike, in Canada, was already on the march. In the spring of 1984 Cobb approved a life company acquisition that would more than double U.S. assets. Similarly, in Canada Mike was giving vent to his acquisitive instincts, buying up life companies and blocks of business. By 1985 the parent company's need for capital was seemingly insatiable. Public issues and private placements took place literally monthly. With the acquisition of the final controlling block of the bank's shares, the Company was now able to remove the fiction of equity accounting and consolidate the assets of the bank into its balance sheet. Assets were ballooning, and it was a propitious moment to use capital markets. The company was on a roll; it seemed in good hands; the team seemed to work. James decided to step down and to transfer all power to the number-two man, Cam.

I interviewed James shortly after he promoted Cam. "Is there anything," I asked, "anything that could jeopardize the future of your firm? Could it be taken over by bureaucrats, for example?" He replied, "No. Its entrepreneurial character is too well entrenched. It's too strongly ingrained in all the people."

Nothing changes overnight, but changes were to come.

CHANGES: 1985 TO 1990

So James disappeared from the power structure and became increasingly isolated. He remained on the board, but both formal and informal power were now in the hands of another man. What kind of man was Cam? As noted earlier, he was a Technocrat. On the map, he's located in the northwest quadrant, opposite James in the southeast. His lowest scores are on humane, amiable, warm, helpful, generous. James chose his opposite to succeed him. Why? Well, for his talents. Cam is serious, cerebral, hardworking, meticulous, determined and methodical. He scores the second highest of all on brilliant. He's conservative, controlled, intense. He seems very sure of himself. Not a man to make many mistakes. Solid, even stolid. Inspires confidence that everything will be under control, everything in its place. No loose ends. Rational choices. Analytic procedures. Sophisticated, in the way that a self-taught man may find himself deficient. When asked why James might have made such a choice, one former executive vice-president stated simply, "He made a mistake; human beings do, you know." James would later rue the day.

THE TEAM: 1986

It is appropriate, now, to pause to get to know the rest of the team, because it was during this brief interlude that a team actually existed. Although the formal power structure saw each of the four group CEOs — Judd, Cobb, Rodney and Robert — reporting directly to the chairman, Cam, the atmosphere of power was much more diffuse. Each of the four held a seat on the nine-man board. James, the previous chairman, was still a member and continued to carry moral weight. The board functioned with little ceremony, more like a management committee than a formal board of governors. Everyone had a say; there was no obvious deference to hierarchical authority. Deals were brought to the table and consensus achieved with little ado. If there was deference at all, they each deferred to one another's right to proceed independently in his sector.

Judd, one of the two senior men James and Cam hired, is a Technocrat; on the map he is positioned within millimetres of the new chairman, Cam, in the northwest quadrant. On the checklists, *no one* calls him volatile, funny, exciting, visionary, intuitive or inspiring. One calls him entrepreneurial. He is quite clearly not an Artist. *No one* calls him honest, humane, people-oriented, wise or open-minded. He is clearly not a Craftsman. On the other hand, a majority calls him controlled, serious, intense, analytical, methodical, and determined. At board meetings, he talks of the progress being made in the merger of his various subsidiaries and the structures and systems that will result from it. He shares with us glowing profit forecasts based on the trends.

As we see in the organizational chart below, reporting to him is Jeb, an archetypal Craftsman; on the map he's in the middle of the craft pack. At the top of the checklists on him are honest and well-balanced, followed immediately by humane, amiable, sensible, dedicated and knowledgeable. He's also predictable and conventional; both admirers and detractors agree on these adjectives. Never cited as difficult, stiff, or hardheaded, he has relationships that are generally harmonious. He is respected and liked by his subordinates, appreciated by the Artists and other Craftsmen and discounted by the Technocrats; at the time, they say things like, "He's weak. We need to get rid of him," or, more subtly, "We have to put someone in there under him to strengthen the analytic capacity." Although seen to be methodical, it isn't enough. Because he is "knowledgeable," has long experience in the business, his presence is, temporarily at least, tolerated.

Moving right in the organizational chart, we find Cobb. Imaginative, bold, inspiring, intuitive, he ties for first place as "exciting." He leaves no one cold or neutral. Overwhelmingly an Artist, he is nonetheless seen by the majority to share the craft virtues: he's honest, humane, people-oriented and open-minded. Indeed, it is just this craft capacity wedded to his artistic vision that makes him "inspiring" in the eyes of his subordinates. There is nothing more gratifying than to be genuinely listened to by someone we consider better than ourselves. One of his immediate subordinates said of him, with deep admiration and affection, "You work for a man like him once in your life." Hard drinker, hard player, ebullient and moody, funny and bold, he flies high, falls low and withdraws — temporarily. He exudes tension. He makes the Technocrats exceedingly uncomfortable. The other Artists alternately conspire with him or, if necessary, try to end-run him to get their way. The Craftsmen chuckle at his histrionics, laugh at his jokes and defer to his vision. They would follow him (almost) anywhere.

Reporting to Cobb, from Canada, is another Artist, Mike. Spiritually fellow-travellers, they sometimes get in each other's way. Dedicated to their own visions, impatient with any procedural delays, neither has much time for approval processes or rules. "There's more than one way to skin a cat" could be their motto. Intuitive and honest, entrepreneurial and generous, daring and dedicated, Mike combines even more strongly the virtues of craft and art. He's visibly calmer than Cobb, but his actions speak otherwise. Like a good thoroughbred, he's classy; "given his head," he takes advantage of it to run free. A Technocrat would say "run wild." He looks after his people, genuinely cares about them. He helps them through difficult personal problems. He is loyal, perhaps to a fault. He is warm, open, laughs readily, smiles regularly. He admits, privately, to recurrent depressive periods, but that is not what the world sees. Not at all arrogant, sometimes naive, he will later be bewildered by events.

Hierarchically Mike's twin, and emotionally his friend, is another Craftsman, Rowan. Amiable, open-minded and sensible, he makes few enemies. Nevertheless, his days are numbered.

Structure mid-1980s

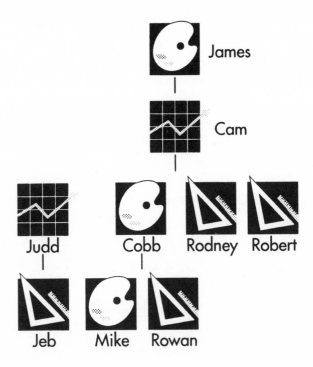

Returning to the level of group CEO, we find two more Craftsmen — Robert and Rodney. Responsible, knowledgeable, trustworthy, reasonable and open-minded, one is quintessentially a Craftsman and the other is positioned as slightly more technocratic on the map. He is seen to be conservative, stronger than conventional. He's more controlled, meticulous, detail-oriented. But, honest and straightforward to a fault, he speaks his mind. Whatever resemblance he has to the Technocrat in cognitive domains, like being meticulous and analytical, will not be able to compensate for the Craftsman sides of his managerial style.

This, then, was the team as the final period of my study opened: led now by a Technocrat, still influenced by a previous Artist chairman, seconded by two Craftsmen, an Artist and a Technocrat. It was an interesting mix. How did they think and what did they do?

STRATEGY AND STYLE

As noted earlier, the strategy of the ensemble had already, with the elevation of Cam to the number-two spot, been evolving in a more well-defined sense. Gone long since were the bits and pieces James had picked up along the way. Now this precision was to intensify; anything not directly connected to financial services was divested. The industry recipe, the conventional wisdom, of participating in all subsections of financial services was followed to the letter. That year's management report was testimony to the new concerns. It read:

> Better-informed consumers, and a growing pool of savings, have brought massive change to the financial services industry. To keep up with this revolution necessitates being able to offer the consumer a broad range of products. In order to manage such a system requires, at the same time, huge continuing investments in information technology. The result is that your organization needs *scale* to defray these costs. The market is irreversibly committed to the integration of services.

Scale is no longer sought in order to accomplish social goals but to reduce costs. This melody began to be played as early as 1983; while James had never been inclined to produce written strategy documents, the elevation of Cam had begun to result in their proliferation. By 1985 the mission statement, conceived centrally and distributed to the divisions, came close but did not use the then-prevailing vocabulary of one-stop shopping. It asserted:

> The group is actively seeking to establish or to join existing distribution networks to reach more consumers. It is planning to develop a national brokerage network to promote the sale of life and general insurance products on an integrated basis. In addition, it is seeking to become associated with retail business firms to test the merchandising of financial services through retail distribution outlets.

Thus the strategy was increasingly clear and well defined. The Craftsmen didn't buy the idea of one-stop shopping for financial services but didn't really care. Interviewed in 1987, one told me, "I just keep my head down and look after business. That's what counts." To him, networking and synergy were theoretical notions and probably, by definition, impracticable. The Artists didn't in any way wish to violate the strategy as stated — unless it got in their way. They largely ignored it, did not pursue the development of similar documents in their own jurisdictions, much to the consternation of the Technocrats, and went about doing what they thought was important — building assets. While the assets of the Technocrat's sector remained steady, the artistically controlled sector ballooned. Quintupling in Canada, doubling in the U.S., overall the sector trebled.

DEVELOPMENTS

Although London-based, Cobb was almost never at head office. Spending half of his time on the Concorde, he was regularly in Canada or the U.S., called upon to be part of acquisition negotiations. When he was home, he was busy with his own deals. In 1987 a broker approached him with the rumour that a certain retail chain in the U.K. would be open to a proposition to join forces with a financial-services company. Cobb recommended a second strategic alliance. This became the fifth major axis of development, paralleling the Sears experiment in the U.S., and someone had to run it. Too busy with offshore and domestic developments, Cobb was persuaded that it should be supervised by someone else. One of his vice-presidents, Bill, was promoted into the slot. Bill was a Craftsman with artistic leanings. Honest, humane, never distant, uncompromising or detail-oriented, he was sometimes seen to be funny, emotional and entrepreneurial. He was to report through the Technocrat, Judd, to the chairman; this because, they said, Judd was based at head office and had "more time." Bill was less than pleased to report to Judd — he knew him — but he wanted the challenge.

CENTRALIZATION/DECENTRALIZATION

Although the ethic and the official language of the group had been decentralist — let the divisions and their independent boards run their own show— there were forces at work moving in the opposite direction. First of all, there was sheer size. As the group grew and diversified, both nationally and internationally, the centre felt cut off from the action yet globally responsible for it. Secondly, the strategy itself, of participating in all subsectors of the financial-services industry, seemed to some to carry with it the necessity of synergy; that is, if you sell general insurance to a client, you may also sell life insurance or a mutual fund. Thus, the various units must be capable of cooperating, and this was a delicate and complex question involving, among other things, complicated systems of sales remuneration. Thirdly, there was a power struggle; would the centre be most important, or would divisional management and their independent boards? This struggle, not at all unique to this particular group, was fed by personal jealousies and by fundamental stylistic differences between the players. Thus, an Artist said of Cameron, "He always talked decentralization. That was what was *expected*. But his actions were always centralizing." To a Technocrat, with his deep-seated need for orderliness and control, decentralization spelled anarchy, and this he could not abide. Given to intellectualization as a primary defence mechanism, he found in the first two factors — size and synergy — the perfect justification for his actions. All these issues were to come to a head around technology.

Servicing an increasingly diverse and demanding clientele meant massive investments in information technology. Synergy, it was argued, necessitated that those investments be harmonized, that all systems be made compatible. Separate systems development would involve huge outlays, possible duplication, higher than necessary operating costs and potential frustration of the synergy objective. Freed from the daily management of his own sector by the presence of a dependable Craftsman and physically lodged at head office, Judd found it logical to assume responsibility for technological harmonization. It was also "logical" that the divisions would fight Judd's assumption. The Craftsmen and Artists running those divisions saw his move very clearly as an incursion into their operating authority, as a restriction on their capacity to innovate in an area vital to competitive advantage and as a patent power play. They also believed that the future of information systems was toward distributed processing. Who was right? In any case, this was not really a contest of facts. In a 1987 interview, one Craftsman offered an explanation: "[Judd] doesn't care about costs or about synergy. He's simply trying to increase his empire and his power." Backed one hundred percent by Cameron, Judd was to succeed in divesting the divisions of important areas of discretion.

What was true for technology was also true, but to a lesser extent and with much smaller financial and discretionary implications, for marketing. Synergy required tapping in to the client databases of each subsidiary and developing common marketing approaches. In this case, a VP at head office, reporting to Judd, played an encouraging role, not a dictatorial one. Nonetheless, any hesitancy or apparent lack of enthusiasm on the part of divisional management did not go unnoticed.

Synergy meant that plans were needed, indeed insisted upon. A head-office executive, once again under Judd's supervision, was given responsibility to "work with the subsidiaries" to develop written strategic five-year plans which could be "harmonized." All but one division, run by a recalcitrant Artist, cooperated; of strategic plans he said:

> They wanted five-year plans, but that stuff's just an excuse not to work. All they do is produce tons of paper that just goes into a shredder eventually, anyway, so what's the point? Can these guys produce and sell a product? No, they say in their plans, "We will produce and sell such and such a product," but they can't do it.

He would later pay for his intransigence. Once a year, a two-day planning retreat was organized, not to consult the divisions but to make sure everyone was "on side" with head office.

All this planning activity spurred an intensification of divestitures. If it didn't exactly correspond to plan, an activity was divested. There was no time to waste on watching dreams grow up. Thus, in this period, assets accumulated in one sector were more than compensated by divestitures in another, such that, overall, asset growth remained almost flat. This divestiture activity was steered by head office and by, guess who, Judd.

Gone now were the days when the annual reports talked philosophy, humanity, love and friendship. With increasing regularity, new words began to replace them. Instead of "friendship," it was "efficiency"; instead of "love," it was "rationalization" and "economies of scale" (emphases are mine):

> In our search for greater *efficiency*, the collaboration of our various companies has brought great benefit. . . . Putting finance and human

> resources functions together allows us to benefit both from *scale* economies and from the possibility of the latest technological advances.
>
> From the point of view of *rationalization*, we have proceeded with the reorganization of [company X], with the sale of [company Y] and we continue to concentrate on *coordinating* technology and marketing.

Coordinating indeed. By now, the areas of finance, human resources, information-systems development and data processing, planning and marketing were all being "coordinated." Coordination was a euphemism for control, and control was a euphemism for centralization. Its byproduct was demoralization.

MANAGEMENT STYLE

The need now to have formal plan approval from the centre gave scope for more intimate inquiry into the managerial style in the operating divisions. One Craftsman put in his mission statement that his organization should be, among other things, "a place to have fun." He added his intention to create the position VP of the Impossible. Cam was far from amused. Both were removed from the mission statement. In another sector, a Craftsman decided on a regular schedule of visits to all his sales outlets — management by walking around. Cam considered this a "complete waste of time"; in the eyes of the chairman this man had more important things to do than to go around talking with staff. One of those "more important things" was to produce profit.

The pace of acquisition activity, although exciting on the street and stimulating for the price of the stock, was not without its downside. It took time, effort and a great deal of money to weld the various units into workable teams — always more time, more effort and more money than forecast. And acquisitions were not always successful. One in Canada was proving disastrous, draining the surpluses normally generated from that region. Convinced that the stock price would follow quarterly earnings and not growth prospects, Cam and his spiritual sidekick Judd began a campaign to boost short-term profits. The emphasis, in planning documents, began to be placed not on long-term development, but on return on investment (ROI) targets. What began as an exercise in harmonization of visions ended in marching orders: produce sixteen percent ROI or get out. A Craftsman insisted, with disdain, "Sixteen percent ROI by 1995 is a joke; we'll be dead by 1995."

That wasn't in the script, but it was in the cards.

Seven

Climax: The Triumph of Technocratic Illusions

For considerable periods the four oboe players had nothing to do. The number should be reduced and the work spread more evenly over the whole of the concert, thus eliminating peaks of activity. All the twelve violins were playing identical notes; this seems unnecessary duplication. The staff of this section should be drastically cut. . . . No useful purpose is served by repeating on the horns a passage which has already been handled by the strings. It is estimated that if all redundant passages were eliminated the whole concert time of 2 hours could be reduced to 20 minutes and there would be no need for an interval.[1]

Cam was by now beginning to feel that he had "too much on his plate"; in particular, the regulatory authorities in all the jurisdictions were very active and required constant watching. As the visible representative of the corporation, the chairman not surprisingly found this responsibility falling largely on his shoulders. In addition, he was feeling his age. Anxious to provide for an eventual smooth succession, he felt it was time to move one of the managing directors into the number-two spot. His choice lay between an Artist, Cobb, running by far the largest operation, and the Technocrat, his head-office sidekick, Judd. It came as no surprise to anyone that Cam chose Judd. "They're birds of a feather; they flock together," commented one Craftsman. "The handwriting has been on the wall for some time," added another disillusioned Craftsman.

Thus, midway through this last period, the organizational structure looked like this:

Structure late 1980s

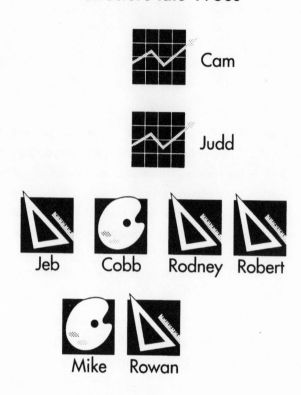

Cam

Judd

Jeb Cobb Rodney Robert

Mike Rowan

PROFITS: THE NEW "STRATEGY"

With two Technocrats at the top, the interest in synergy began curiously to wane. It was time to get serious. Maybe this synergy business was a distraction; the thing to concentrate on was running each core business to the best of everyone's ability. A Technocrat described it in the following terms:

> In James's day, it was a cult of personality. Things happened without him realizing it. In the sense that it was all *opportunistic*. There was *no strategy*.

Why were they in Canada, the U.S.? It all lacked *logic*. Then they brought in the pros, Cam and Judd, to put some *order* into it all. They built the group around a concept that does not work — synergy. One-stop shopping, like a drugstore. But, there has been no revolution, just evolution. Everybody is just getting better at what they do in individual sectors.

But synergy had been what everyone said was necessary; it was the conventional wisdom of the day. But a new era had begun — the era that said "stick to your knitting," so now the Technocrats turned to it. The Craftsmen, who had always stuck to their knitting, were amused by this new turn of phrase, but not amused by what would then be erected in its name. Getting better meant getting more profitable. Right now. Today.

THE CANADIAN SCENE

Once contributing substantial profits to the group as a whole, Canadian operations were now a drain on cash flow. A two-year-old acquisition had gone badly awry. The due diligence at the time of acquisition had been badly flawed, and the underlying assets turned out to be in much greater disrepair than imagined. It was haemorrhaging cash. Mike, the Artist in charge there, was under considerable heat, as was his London boss, Cobb, since Canadian operations were consolidated into Cobb's sector's earnings statements. Mike kept asking for time; Cobb was blamed for giving it to him. Formally now Cobb's boss, Judd insisted that Cobb place someone in charge "over there" who knew what he was doing. To Judd, that meant a technician, an actuary, an accountant, a finance guy. Mike was temporarily kicked upstairs, removed from day-to-day operating authority and, within six months, fired.

Cobb:

> I shielded Mike for a long time, but I couldn't do it indefinitely. He was resisting. Talking back too much. He always said what he thought and that was very dangerous. They never had patience

with investments. They panic. At that time, I couldn't stave off their assault. My own power base was too weak.

Mike:

It wasn't Cobb's fault. It was those guys'. They have a total disrespect for skills, experience. Even when I was a kid I sought out older people to listen to. They think whiz kids can run anything. There's no tolerance for error. Trial and error is how you learn. If they had let me solve that haemorrhage I could have stopped loss. But no, they had decided that I created the problem so I couldn't solve it. It was the excuse they needed. They were just waiting for me to fall. I should have seen it but I didn't. I just couldn't believe they could be so stupid. I used to pray before meetings, "Please, God, help me to keep my mouth shut," but it never worked. They wanted five-year plans, but that stuff's just an excuse not to work. All they do is produce tons of paper that just goes into a shredder eventually, anyway, so what's the point? Can these guys produce and sell a product? No, they say in their plans, "We will produce and sell such and such a product," but they can't do it. They don't know salesmen. They can't stand them. Me, I honour them. I treasured what they did. You have to love what you do to do it well. They don't love anything. Me, I went on my instincts. Ninety-nine percent of the time it worked; I made one mistake. I'm out. But what will they do now? They've picked all the fruit from the tree to artificially inflate earnings. What will they do now? There's no fresh air. They're like the Russian technocrats, destroyers. That's why Russia's crumbling. Parasites living off the productivity of others and ultimately destroying that which they live off. . . . Okay, I screwed up, but do they ever admit they've done anything wrong? For them, people have to be perfect, all assets, no liabilities. It's so unrealistic.

In this *cri de coeur* we hear the Artist's disdain for planning exercises; he paid for that. We hear the belief in instincts; he paid for that, too. We hear once again words like we heard from James — love, honour, treasure.

Cam:

> You know it's the only thing I regret; I should never have let him buy that company. I had strong doubts, but he was so insistent. It's too bad.

Cam had been the chairman of Mike's board. Ultimately the acquisition was *his* responsibility, but he accepts none. What we don't hear from Cam is more important than what we hear. Cam is not remorseful about the firing. Mike made a mistake and as surely as night follows day had to be fired for it. He regrets, instead, not having maintained a fail-safe system, not having *controlled* the situation.

A board member:

> They should never have fired Mike, but he was just like James and Cobb. Generate new ideas and get on with it. Entrepreneurial personalities, impulsive, opportunistic. But Cam was not . . . I don't know, maybe it's a phase. You know, growth, passion, followed by a period of reorganization ad nauseam, then a new growth phase. But the only way growth will happen is if there is a hostile takeover; it's not these guys who will create new opportunities.

Mike was replaced by a Technocrat.

THE UNITED STATES

The acquisition that had, in one coup, doubled U.S. assets had also doubled Rowan's headaches. Head office had to be moved into larger quarters. Sales teams' pre-merger compensation packages were completely different. Accounting systems were not up to handling the extra load. "Things got lost." Computer systems were incompatible and too small. There was no control, or at least seemed not to be. Profits were adequate but below expectations. Post-merger economies took their jolly good time materializing. In short, a mess.

Rowan was a Craftsman. He believed these things would take time but would eventually sort themselves out. He didn't feel he could push the system any harder than it was already being pushed; that could create worse problems — discontented salesmen, diminished production, morale problems. These things simply take time. It's *unrealistic* to think otherwise.

Rowan:

> I don't know why it happened. Profits were on budget; bonuses were paid. I guess they just wanted more. The spotlight began to shine on us when things started to go badly over there. I guess they needed us to compensate for it. They wanted everything faster and more, but there was no time. They didn't really understand our situation over here. Too distant from the coalface to understand how the business works. Gave them exaggerated expectations. In person, everything was sweetness and light. I suppose they're honest, but they're certainly not straightforward. Now the whole group is like an individual with a frontal lobotomy. No memory. They've sacked anyone who knows anything about the business. They don't respect experience. They hire based on type, and type is somebody who will do the work without raising any objections, any implied criticism. They have a clear view of management style and anything else is aberrant. Nobody who wants to make a mark will ever succeed with them. Their strategy was very murky. They seemed only to be fascinated by tinkering with the thing — structures, systems. Now they've used up all the goodies, the organization is really anorexic. They seemed to think that you could grow and expand and not have an impact on the bottom line. But any schoolboy knows better. They're like the little old lady who says, "I want capital gains and income." Totally unrealistic.

Here we hear again the Craftsman's bewilderment. How could they think that the system of people could be pushed any harder? He who values straightforwardness, honesty, realism, finds the Technocrat unreasonable, unrealistic, even childish in his managerial theories, a man with a child's dogmatism.

Judd on Rowan:

> He simply was not a manager. He was over his head. He was an adviser. He was volatile, unpredictable, imaginative, visionary. A nice guy, very amiable. The kind of guy you might seek ideas from but not the guy to run something. Didn't know how to work.

Judd gives us a very typical Technocrat's response. To him, Rowan was a very likable guy. He had nothing personal against him. There is no affect, no emotion, involved here; it's simply a matter of judgement and being realistic. Rowan couldn't do the job; he had to go. Nothing personal. No hard feelings. Note, as well, his suggestion that Rowan was not a hard worker, a suggestion contradicted by others closer to the scene. Judd expects a managing director to give 150 percent of his time to work. Leisure is a luxury.

A board member on Rowan:

> He was very well mannered and considerate. He fired people but did it nicely. He was hardworking and very dedicated. Very open-minded. Sometimes ahead of his time. I don't know what they wanted.

Rowan was replaced by a Technocrat.

THE UNITED KINGDOM

The profit and loss statements of Canada and the U.S. were consolidated directly into Cobb's financial statements. The stock market crash of 1987 was having a negative impact on his earnings, even though the losses could be amortized over several years. This made him more vulnerable. In addition, Cobb's handling of the U.S. and

Canadian situations, or what was more the prevailing view, his failure to handle them, confirmed opinions about his "managerial capacity." "He's just not a manager," they said. It had not helped, of course, that he was less than enthusiastic about "harmonizing" the information technologies or marketing, or synergies. And it had not helped that he was the only other serious contender for the top spot. It was decided that he needed "assistance," a more "professional" man under him. This pro was to have a seat on his board, become the managing director, and Cobb was to be kicked upstairs, where "his talents could be put to better use." Cobb had seen this pattern before. He knew very well what it meant. Ross, another Technocrat, was to take over.

A board member:

> As soon as Judd won, Cobb lost heart. It was, of course, compounded by the arrival of Ross and his perpetual past run-ins with Cam, but basically the die was cast. He had to go. There was no way to stop the momentum. There was no way he could get along with them.

Cobb's own board didn't like it — there was a minor and futile revolt — but as another board member put it, "What the shareholder wants, the shareholder gets." Judd and his man Ross, a Technocrat, were in; Cobb was out.

In general, the Technocrats liked Cobb, or so they said. They call him intuitive, imaginative, visionary, in short, all the artistic features that make up his personality. He just couldn't do the job.

A Technocrat:

> He was Startrecky. He produced a hundred new ideas but only one of them would be useful. It's terribly inefficient and ineffective. The people underneath get frustrated. It's awe-inspiring but eventually demotivating. Our world cannot do without them but our organizations can.

A Craftsman identifies the nature of the "mistake" Cobb made:

> He was the visionary, spent his time on acquisitions and foreign operations and wrongly trusted his staff to run the show at home. But he never implemented the head-office system that would have allowed the decentralized management of the subsidiaries. So the wheels started falling off all the carts.

Cobb:

> It was all about strategy. What is strategy anyway? Grand plan? No. You try to instill a vision you have and get people to buy in. The strategy comes from astrology, quirks, dreams, love affairs, science fiction, perception of society, some madness probably, ability to guess. It's clear but fluid. Action brings precision. Very vague but becomes clear in the act of transformation. Creation is the storm. They always built things around "barring unforeseen circumstances," but that doesn't leave room for the unforeseen. It implies you know the future. It's a straightjacket, narrow walls. The unforeseen is not supposed to exist, but you have unforeseen government policy, economic change, fraud, loss of key people, technological change. These people live outside of reality. You should never allow the plumber to be the engineer, because he'll run the pipes across the top of your machines because it will be easier and cheaper to repair later. Of course, in the meantime, people can't work.

Around the same time, two Craftsmen, Rodney and Robert, also lost their jobs. The Technocrats said things like: "They just couldn't do the job"; "He didn't evolve with the times"; "He was too old-fashioned"; "He wasn't tough enough"; "He was boring"; "He has no personality." They were replaced by David, a Technocrat, and by George, a Craftsman (a mistake they would later correct). The latter was to find himself exceedingly uncomfortable in the days to come.

A Craftsman (with an MBA):

> Their kind strip the essence out of organizations, empty them of their sense. I think it's a product of the engineers and MBAs of the 80s, the technocratic mentality. But everywhere it's proved a failure. People are beginning to see it.

During this period, the tenor of public statements changed, as well. The preoccupation with reorganization, rationalization, consolidation, structures and profit was intensified:

> We are proceeding with the reinforcement [read, firing] of our management teams, with the rebalancing of our activities, and an intense effort of rationalization [read, cutting] of our operations. We are also proceeding with a revision of our operating structures [read, new organization charts] in order to promote the achievement of our objectives and improve our performance [read, quarterly profits].

The next year, the same themes were played:

> The progress observed in our results is the fruit of several changes: the reinforcement of our management teams, the rationalization of operations and the concentration of activities.

A New Man at the Helm

By the end of the 1985–1990 period, Cameron had vacated the chair in favour of Judd, over the objections of significant minority shareholders on his board.

A board member:

> We tried everything we could to stop it, but he wouldn't listen. He's stubborn. He just didn't want to hear and, short of a proxy war, there was nothing to be done. Besides, there was no longer any other potential candidate inside. We'll just have to wait.

Eventually they'll make a mistake. Things will continue to go badly and we'll be there to pick up the pieces.

Another board member:

> I went to him at the time because I felt sure he was going to choose Judd. I was not necessarily in favour of Cobb; I wasn't sure that he was the right man either. But at the worst, we should recruit outside. I didn't trust Judd; he always seemed to say the right thing at the right time and that made me very uneasy. I didn't think he had the intelligence or the depth to run an organization of this size and complexity. Cam was very defensive, even angry. He said that Judd was brilliant, that he had turned around his sector, and that was that. I was ushered out of his office.

I asked Cam if Judd had ever disagreed with him about anything. "No," he said, "but what has that got to do with anything?" (The Technocrat is submissive *until* he gets into power; this is symptomatic of the compulsive personality, remember? Relations organized around dominance and submission.)

With Judd's elevation, the organization looked like the following chart. The Artists — James, Mike and Cobb — were all gone. So were the Craftsmen — Rowan, Rodney and Robert. Two other Craftsmen, George and Bill, were demoted, a third, Jeb, knew he was next. He was to be lent assistance by a new recruit —- to all appearances, another Technocrat. In fact, in the closing days of the study, Jeb was kicked upstairs and was on his way out. (He would be fired a year later.) In the end, only Technocrats had any power or influence.

Structure 1990

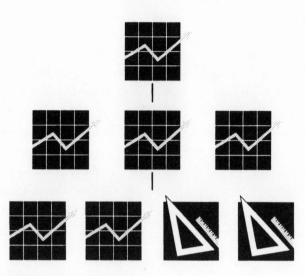

STRATEGY

A report concluded:

> Mirroring a worldwide trend among large financial groups, we initiated in 1989 and continued in 1990 an extensive program under which operations were regrouped, assets sold and activities rationalized. As a result, we now operate in two sectors: insurance and banking. . . . New chief executives have been appointed and our strategy is profitability.

"Our strategy is profitability"; many felt this formulation was a contradiction in terms. Profitability is an outcome, not a strategy. Asked what the current strategy was, one remaining Craftsman replied, "I honestly don't know." A relatively new Technocrat said, "I wish I knew. They seem to concentrate on short-term profits. I guess that is a strategy. There's a meeting coming up. Maybe then I'll know more." He didn't. But that doesn't matter because he has since been fired. Another Technocrat, closer to the centre and part of the "action," adds,

"Eventually? Alliances. *Everybody knows* [read, you imbecile] you have to create alliances. In the meantime, we've had to create profit." The new buzzword is strategic alliances; it is on all their lips.

A Craftsman:

They don't know. Billions have been spent on strategic planning, but that's not the issue. It's strategic thinking. The plan comes later. It fits into the "profile" of what you want to be when you grow up. James and Cobb had the "profile," the vision. Strategic planning is the death knell of strategic thinking. Once it's on paper, the job's done! Even if they had a vision, how would they get it done? There's no managerial continuity. At this year's planning meeting, there were four out of fourteen people left over from 1988. Every two years there's a new chief executive. There's no opportunity to fail, so there's no continuity. They focus directly on profit, but they'll never get it because profit comes from the vision and the people, and they won't invest in people. If you look after the people, the profit follows. You can't drive at it directly. Sixteen percent ROI is a joke; we'll be dead by 1995. They refuse to see this. You can't correct a problem unless you see it exists. It's like me. I look in the mirror and I see a young fullback, not a balding, middle-aged man with his chest on his belly. You have to see *reality* to change it.

THE NEW "TEAM"

The Technocrats view each other:

He's a lightweight. They all are. Amateurs.

People are too hard on him. He's not a lightweight. It's true he's not brilliant, but he's put order into the shop.

He's an ass.

Not much team spirit there!

Technocrats on previous eras:

> In James's day it was easy. Things moved slowly and you could afford to make mistakes. Now when you make a mistake you know it instantly and the consequences are much bigger. You just can't take those risks now.

Technocrats always feel that the past was simple and that their times are more complex and difficult and demand their much greater sophistication. They are narcissistic.

> James, Cobb, Rowan, they were all dreamers, not entrepreneurs, not builders. They're what I call advisers. Now we have builders. They're conservative, of course, but if you're not conservative you'll lose everything. James was always talking in metaphors. It took a professional like Cam to put some order into things.

Well, the organization started full of optimism and reached out to the world. It grew and consolidated by art and by craft. Now, it had lots of *order* and was full of *professionals*, all watching the systems and the bottom line. But the Craftsman who told me in 1990, "Sixteen percent ROI by 1995 is a joke; we'll be dead by 1995," was wrong. As I sit here at my computer today, in February 1994, James's dream is already stone-cold dead. The vision, and the organization it spawned and nurtured, collapsed. With poor profit performance and a stock trading at less than half book value, the company was easy prey for a takeover. Some people escaped from the wreckage without a scratch. But there were many casualties, and some lives were damaged irreparably.

Let's examine why.

Eight Dénouement: The Collapse of Vision

> We are as ambivalent about heroism as we are about the workaday goals that it sacrifices. We struggle to hold on to a vision of the incomparably higher, while being true to the central modern insights about the value of ordinary life. We sympathize with both the hero and the anti-hero; and we dream of a world in which one could be in the same act both.
>
> CHARLES TAYLOR, *THE SOURCES OF THE SELF*[1]

What does this fifteen-year story tell us? I'm sure you have your own ideas, and that is as it should be; everyone hears different music in the same recording. Here's what I hear.

I think there are a lot of reasons for the collapse. Some argue that there's been a big "shakeout" in financial institutions — U.S. savings and loans institutions, Canadian trust companies and insurers, for example. Well, that's true, but why was this particular group shaken out? What made it, and not another, more subject to, more vulnerable to, these forces?

Another argument often proposed is that the group was "overextended," that it got carried away by acquisition euphoria and had to pay the piper. Well, okay, but let's look closely at this argument. It's certainly true that first James, and then Cobb and Mike with James's moral support, believed that the primary goal was to build a strong enough asset base to be able to compete globally. Cobb argues that you have to shoot high to attain your goals, because there is inevitable slippage from them. On the back of an envelope, he drew a diagram for me:

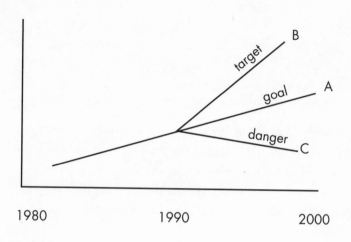

Here's how he explained it:

> Say you have a goal for the year 2000. You have to shoot at a target, point B, much higher than the goal, point A, in order even to come close, because the world is always changing — competition, obsolescence, government, deaths. So, you acquire, you do R&D, you look for new markets. If you drive directly at the goal (A), you will inevitably fall short and arrive at point C. The cost-cutters think they're driving at the goal, but all the while they've got their heads down looking at the books, the whole world changes around them and the whole thing collapses. At 1990, the two approaches may look the same, but by the year 2000, it looks different.

This is the Artists' explanation for the collapse. Too much time and energy had been devoted to structures, to reorganizations, to systems, to short-term profits, and too little time devoted to development of new products and new markets.

You might reply that this was inevitable. The group was big — £10 billion in assets — and these centralized systems *had* to be developed.

But why? There was no profitability problem in James's day. James didn't need elaborate centralized control mechanisms, because he left the discretion in other people's hands. He let the CEOs run their businesses. He sat on their boards and sometimes asked embarrassing questions. But basically, the various divisions ran their own shows. He believed they were better at it, knew more about their business than he did. He trusted them. Furthermore, he had other castles to build. The Artist *always* has new ideas, new projects; it's his nature, his *character*.

Yes, but "synergy," you say. Synergy necessitated making them all work together. Well, so it was thought at the time. It was certainly the conventional wisdom. But within three years synergy was judged no longer necessary, so I have a hard time believing that it was logical, a rule carved in stone. Carved in paper mâché maybe. Even the Technocrats abandoned the rationale once they'd used it to achieve their centralizing goals. They *need* to centralize, do you see? They will use any intellectualization, any handy excuse, to get it. They're *frightened*. They're afraid of failing. They believe that only *they* possess *Truth*. Only *they* know how to do things. Only *they* are competent. This is their nature, their *character*.

The Craftsman agrees with this diagnosis, says the group collapsed because there was too much "tinkering with the thing." But the Craftsman adds another, and in his mind more vital, reason. "Now the whole group is like an individual with a frontal lobotomy. No memory. They've sacked anyone who knows anything about the business." The Craftsman believes you can't run something unless you have experience. You will inevitably make clumsy, unnecessary mistakes. You will, by this clumsiness, by this lack of skill and dexterity, alienate and undermine traditional markets. You can't stick to your knitting if you don't know what knitting needles look like.

The Craftsman also believes that, even if you have a good strategy, you have to work through and with experienced people to get the job done. He thinks, therefore, that continuity of personnel is the *sine qua non* of bringing the vision to fruition. One told us:

> Even if they had a vision [which they don't], how would they get it done? At last year's planning meeting, there were only four out of fourteen people left over from 1988. Every two years there's a new chief executive.

New people brought on board continually have to learn the business from scratch, particularly, as was usually the case, when they don't come from the industry —"They think whiz-kids can run anything."

But why is there no continuity? Because Technocrats can't allow mistakes; Mike said, "Okay, I screwed up, but do they ever admit they've done anything wrong? For them, people have to be perfect, all assets, no liabilities. It's so unrealistic." If you ask the Technocrat, he'll tell you this is not true. He knows, better than most, all the management literature. He's the one who reads it. He knows all about "empowerment," all about "loyalty," all about "participative management." He knows, theoretically, that you have to allow people to make mistakes. He can give you learned discourses on these subjects. Judd gave me a long lecture one day on "total quality management" and how it was the new secret to success, to "empower" people. This was, it goes without saying, after he had gotten rid of all the "dreamers" and the "incompetents" and replaced them with "professionals."

In Chapter Three, I told you that walking into this organization was like walking into a morgue. Well, in one way it was, but not in another — there are no cadavers hanging around the halls. Actually, nobody hangs around the halls. Nonetheless, the absent — the people who left or were fired — make themselves felt. There's an atmosphere of tension and fear. "Who will be next?" "Will it be me?" "Am I 'professional' enough?" One Craftsman told me, "I'm trying to turn myself into a robot, but I'm not succeeding very well." As a result, people work to rule; that is, they do nothing that might later be construed as a mistake. They stop taking any risks. And they look for other jobs. Those who are not fired leave voluntarily. There's a haemorrhage of experience. Although the Craftsman is not "brilliant," he sees this haemorrhage and its implications very clearly. He's wise. That is his nature, his *character*.

In my books, the vision collapsed because there were no Artists left, no new "bridges thrown out toward an unseen shore"; all the shores were too well defined. According to the Technocrats, the Artists weren't to be trusted; they were fools and dreamers. And there were no Craftsmen left to engineer and build the bridges. Craftsmen were caught in the cross fire; insufficiently glamorous, insufficiently visionary, on the one hand, and insufficiently rigorous on the other. They couldn't win against the technocratic juggernaut. So all that was left was just a bunch of technicians, virtuosos, paint-by-numbers managers. But management is not paint-by-numbers art. If it were, we wouldn't be in such confusion today.

THE TECHNOCRATIC TRIUMPH

But how did they do it, these Technocrats? Why were they so powerful? How could they succeed in getting rid of everybody? One, they're brilliant. They really are. Minds like steel traps. They come into board meetings with their five-part plans and strategies and projections, with their slogans, their grandiloquence and their recipes, and it's pretty impressive stuff. It's intimidating to ordinary mortals. By high-jacking the language of vision, by imitating it, they seem brilliant. Apart from their technical skill and ingenuity, their virtuosity, these *grands parleurs* (big talkers) have something else: they're *strategic about human relationships*.

Whether by Machiavellian intention or by the necessity of their characters, they think very long-term about human relationships.[2] They undermine others gradually. They start by making fun of someone or of his ideas:

> (*Friendly chuckle*) James? Well, that's James (*chuckle, wink*). He cares about those kinds of things. You know, emotional, sentimental. But don't worry, we follow up behind him and look after the serious stuff.

But of course, you can't get rid of someone who has the status of folk hero, so you manoeuvre him into leaving of his own accord. After you have insidiously undermined his credibility, first by implying that he's not to be taken seriously and then by indicating that modern management demands something more sophisticated (by the way, did you know that sophisticated originally meant "spoil the simplicity or purity or naturalness of"?[3]), you gradually remove him from power. Judd and Cam, ever so gradually, removed James from all the important operating boards and committees. I sat across from James one day at a luncheon during which a list of new appointments was announced. His name was no longer on the list. He leaned over to me and whispered, "They could have told me before the meeting, don't you think? Just as a courtesy?" But no. He might have kicked up a fuss. They might have had to defend themselves publicly. James had literally made these men's careers. He built the empire; he hired them; he handed them power and they used it to stab him in the back. They pushed him and pushed him to the limits, and finally he had no choice but to resign. With him gone the rest was easy.

Isolation is another tactic Technocrats use to great advantage. You pick them off one guy at a time. No mass firings, just sniper fire. First, you undermine someone's credibility by mocking it; second, you imply that he needs (poor fellow) help; then you install "help" under him; then you kick him upstairs where his "talents can be put to better use"; then, what do you know, "It's not working out. He's going to have to go"; finally you pay him a big separation settlement and he's gone and you move on to the next one. After Mike was fired, I said to Rowan, "Watch your back. You're next." He said, "What do you mean?" You see, he just couldn't believe it. It was like a nightmare, and he was sure he'd wake up and people would have come to their senses. It's an old rule, no? Divide and conquer.

But the board! you say. Where was the main board of directors? Surely it could see the pattern. Some members did, but they were in a distinct minority, especially since Judd and Cam had loaded the board increasingly with friends and doubled its numbers. More importantly, however, each incident seemed isolated, minor, justified. The new members couldn't see the pattern because they hadn't been around long enough to see patterns in anything. They didn't know the executives who were being rounded up and corralled. Even the old-timers, like the one who said "They should never have fired Mike," didn't say anything publicly because he knew that he himself would be gone the next day if he spoke up. He was still clinging to the faint hope of being able to use his influence to minimize the damage. It's fine, in retrospect, to criticize him, but at the time his motives and his intelligence were both beyond reproach. He didn't have any *power*. No one else did. The decks were all stacked. The dice were all loaded. The game was crooked.

About That Nasty Word "Power"

What really happened here was one colossal mistake, and James was the one who made it. He knows this now. "It's all my fault. I'm the one that put Cam in power." The thing about Artists and Craftsmen is that they admit to their mistakes. That's life. That's what humans do. They make mistakes. Sometimes small and sometimes big. But to James's everlasting regret — he's heartsick about what happened — this was a big one. The selection of one wrong man led to the destruction of everything he built.

James, an Artist, chose his opposite to succeed him. He was naive about Cam. Remember his response to my question at the time? "Could the organization be taken over by bureaucrats?" "No," he said. "Its entrepreneurial character is too well entrenched. It's too strongly ingrained in all the people." Apparently not in all the people. James got fooled, but he got fooled for very good reason. The Technocrat is submissive, even obsequious, with his bosses, but authoritarian with his subordinates. The Technocrat is a chameleon;

he changes colour depending on the surroundings. In the early eighties, the Technocrats trumpeted their entrepreneurship; it was then conventional wisdom. They were surrounded by entrepreneurs. In the mid-eighties, they trumpeted their managerial sophistication with "synergy" and "one-stop shopping" for financial services. It was conventional wisdom; all the "experts" said it was the right thing to do. In the late eighties, the trend was to "rigour," the "bottom line," "stick to your knitting," so that's what they did. They competed for how many people they could lay off. Today they're preaching "reengineering," "total quality management," "empowerment" and "strategic alliances." This last they particularly like because to them it means getting in bed with a big, strong partner who can protect them from a very scary world.

James never *talked* about "strategic alliances." He didn't even know the term because it hadn't yet been invented when, thirty years ago, he created one with EFC. He *did* deals; he didn't *talk* about them. He didn't talk about trusting people or about decentralization, either. He just *did* it. It was second nature to him. And all the Craftsmen — Rodney and Robert and Jeb and the others — they didn't *talk* about "empowerment" or "total quality management" or "learning organizations" or "mentoring" or any other fancy recipes. They just *did* it. It was second nature to them. As Osborne had told us in an earlier chapter, craftsmanship is all about a *cult of excellence*. You don't have to tell a Craftsman to be concerned about the quality of his product or his service. It comes as easily to him as breathing. It's how he lives his life. In fact, maybe it's no accident that all sorts of recipes for quality, learning, empowerment, participation, teamwork, mentoring and so on have proliferated during a time of universal technocratic triumph; we have had to reinvent what the craftsman assures naturally.

In any case, Cam didn't repeat James's mistake; if he had appointed his opposite to succeed him, some equilibrium might have been restored. But no. Technocrats, when they value anyone at all, only value other Technocrats. Only Technocrats are competent. Thus,

Cam appointed Judd, and the two together chased out all the others and installed five more *competent* clones — or, let us say, quasi-clones, because a couple of them were quite emotional and volatile (of the blast furnace variety). The organization tipped fatally toward disequilibrium — like a boat that takes on water when everyone leans to one side.

This happened because power cannot be distributed equally. It may not be politically correct to say so, but some people don't deserve power. They're dangerous. They abuse it, and not just obvious sickos like Hitler. Some basically moral people are blind. They can't help it. And they can't be taught because they live in the closed circle of their own logic. Competence, for example, is serious; it's not funny and it's certainly not amiable. They can be taught to say words like "empowerment," and even to believe them, but they can't "walk the talk." The intellectual graft doesn't *take* on the affective tree.

Does all this mean that Technocrats should be marched out and shot at dawn? Of course not. We are all as much to blame as they are. We let them take power. Why? Because we're scared, too, and their formulae are very reassuring to us. They seem to know the way to the future. They have a three-part response to every question. We can sink into a comfortable dependency safe in the knowledge that they will look after us, secure our futures. *But it ain't so.* They can't.

And we give them power for all the reasons that philosopher Charles Taylor talks about, although he says it so much better than I could ever hope to do. The social and intellectual reasons. We, as much as the Technocrats, distrust emotion and passion. Passion, of a religious variety, caused the inquisition and certain other, more modern, unspeakable horrors. We distrust dreamers; dreamers can turn out to be madmen.

And tradition, we distrust it, too; clinging to it kept corrupt absolute monarchy in place, and we had to get rid of that. We have lost our respect for craft, except in the flea-market context, because to us it also seems too slow. We want answers and solutions right now, today. There's no time to waste. Have you noticed how everyone says things like, "It's an age of discontinuity," or we are living through a "rupture" or a "crisis," meaning, "Hurry up! Do something!!!" This, too, is inimical to craftsmanship. Every age imagines itself faced with unprecedented rapid changes and turbulent times, and it's just narcissism to imagine that our age is somehow exceptional. Only history can make a relative judgement. In France, a fourteenth-century man stepped outside onto his doorstep one morning to find that half the population of his village had been wiped out by the great plague (in which half the population of Europe was destroyed). He wanted to call on God for help, but didn't know whether to address himself to Rome or to Avignon because two legitimate popes were at war! Not verbal war, real war. As he stepped from the threshold of his hovel, he was assaulted by a marauding band of mercenary soldiers who supported themselves in France by rape and pillage. This was the Middle Ages. Did the man know he was living in the Middle Ages?[4] Of course not. He just lived in Lyon. Did he know that the Renaissance was just around the corner? Of course not. No one did. Did he think the times were turbulent? *You bet.*

That brings me to another point about the confusion and depression in which we find ourselves engulfed. It breeds both dependency and magical thinking and creates an environment in which Technocrats thrive. Do the names Isaiah, Jesus, Mohammed, mean anything to you? Why is it that it has always taken *centuries* to produce a new prophet and this *decade* has produced a gaggle of "futurists" several thousands strong? Nostradamus would be so proud! This must be the first generation in all of human history to know nothing about the past and everything about the future. How can it be true that, whereas all previous generations had to struggle through without knowing the future, our generation does not? Isn't this just magical thinking? Aren't we just so insecure, so desperate, that we give a platform to anybody who claims to know where we're going?

What is this "science" of futurism if not the same one the Technocrat uses? Trend-line projection. You take a trend, say, world fossil-fuel reserves, and extrapolate it. Let's look at an example. Remember how the Club of Rome produced a dramatic report telling the world that the world's reserves of fossil fuel were running out? Pretty soon, they said, there wouldn't be a single drop left. They'd looked at a trend and projected it into the future. Well, the whole world panicked. Governments scrambled to develop plans to deal with the emergency. In Canada, we had a National Energy Policy (NEP), which turned policy upside down, penalized our industry and our western provinces and left permanent interregional scars. OPEC put the price up. High prices stimulated conservation and exploration and substitution. Have you been in a gasoline lineup lately? Reality often surprises trend predictions. Sometimes the publication of trends succeeds in reversing them (like polls during elections, for example) and thus may serve a useful social function. To rely on them for knowing the future, however, is worse than hazardous. Benjamin Franklin: "But in this world nothing can be said to be certain, except death and taxes."

This graph illustrates my point.

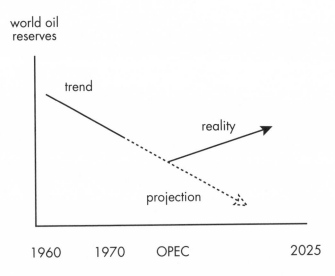

world oil
reserves

trend

reality

projection

1960   1970   OPEC   2025

When I get really down on myself, down on my capacity to run my own life in a satisfactory way, guess what I do? I read my horoscope! I figure, well, I can't run my life, so I might as well turn it over to some magical guidance from the planets. The more depressed I am, the faster I turn to it. But somewhere, deep in the back of my mind, I'm laughing at myself. I *know* this is a joke. I know I will emerge from the depression.

When we are depressed, we become dependent. We look for magical answers — drugs or alcohol, for example. In a social, collective context, we look to futurists (trend-predictors) and/or visionary leaders (trend-setters). We think the Technocrats have misled us — and they have — so we cry out for their opposites, the Artists. We want to flip from one form of dependency to another. This, I think, explains the tremendous upsurge in interest in leadership — and for perversion.

Unfortunately we are, as usual, throwing a great many babies out with a lot of bathwater. I'll have a few things to say about that later, but for now, I want to explore the consequences of this play, the moral of this story, for organizations. To do that, in Part III, I'm going to revisit some current notions about leadership.

III

The Moral of the Story

Nine | Leadership Revisited

To a person who knows his business as scientist, historian, philosopher, or any kind of inquirer, the refutation of a false theory constitutes a positive advance in his inquiry. It leaves him confronted, not by the same old question over again, but by a new question, more precise in its terms and therefore easier to answer. This new question is based on what he has learned from the theory he has refuted. If he has learned nothing, this proves either that he is too foolish (or too indolent) to learn, or that by an unfortunate error of judgment he has been spending time on a theory so idiotic that there is nothing to be learnt from it. Where the refuted theory, even though untrue as a whole, is not completely idiotic, and where the person who has refuted it is reasonably intelligent and reasonably painstaking, the upshot of his criticism can always be expressed in some form as this: "The theory is untenable as regards its general conclusions; but it has established certain points which must henceforth be taken into account."

R.G. COLLINGWOOD, *THE PRINCIPLES OF ART*

That's a very long quotation, but necessary, I think, because what I do *not* intend to do here is explain in great detail what a bunch of fools other analysts have been. Nor am I going to waste my time and yours on "idiotic" theories. Instead, I'm going to take a couple that make a lot of sense and see what I can add to them to make a little more. I'm going to take two of the best and most famous theories of leadership and go through the second one almost line by line.

LEADERSHIP ACCORDING TO ABRAHAM ZALEZNIK

Almost twenty years ago, Harvard's Abraham Zaleznik created for us a distinction between "leaders" and "managers."[1] To wake us up, he painted a stark contrast. Leaders, he argued, were visionary; managers, planners. Leaders cared about substance; managers, about form and process. Leaders inspired; managers motivated. Although his work became famous, to all intents and purposes, it was ignored; his was a lone and courageous voice fighting a tidal wave of what he would later call the "managerial mystique."[2] This mystique, with its pretensions to be a science, with its seemingly dispassionate "hollow men," with its obsession for process over content, for short-term profits, he claimed, was responsible for the decline of American competitive advantage. America had stopped inventing, stopped dreaming and was busy pushing paper around. She needed, desperately, to bring back leaders and get rid of all the managers. Zaleznik wrote:

> The managerial mystique is only tenuously tied to reality. As it evolved in practice, the mystique required managers to dedicate themselves to process, structures, roles and indirect forms of communication and to ignore ideas, people, emotions and direct talk. It deflected attention from the realities of business, while it reassured and rewarded those who believed in the mystique. . . . Essentially, business in America lost its comparative advantage by focusing on profits and stock prices instead of fostering innovation and long-term goals.

Sounds a lot like the Technocrat, no?

AND WARREN BENNIS

Zaleznik, like many wise men, was ahead of his time. But time is catching up with him. Warren Bennis, easily America's foremost expert on leadership, confesses freely to a heavy reliance on Zaleznik's distinction between managers and leaders. In his 1989 book, *On Becoming a Leader*, he produces the following comparative list:

THE MANAGER	THE LEADER
administers	innovates
is a copy	is an original
maintains	develops
focuses on systems and structure	focuses on people
relies on control	inspires trust
has a short-range view	has a long-range perspective
asks how and when	asks what and why
has his eye always on the bottom line	has his eye on the horizon
imitates	originates
accepts the status quo	challenges the status-quo
is the classic good soldier	is his own person
does things right	does the right thing

I claim that this list, however appealing, is misleading. Let me try to explain why.

1) The manager administers; the leader innovates.
"Innovate: from Latin *innovare*, to renew, alter." My Artist certainly innovates on a grand scale. But the Craftsman innovates, renews — albeit on a smaller, more human scale — all the time. He changes tools to suit the new circumstances. The Technocrat innovates, too; he *alters* and claims to renew. Organizations go through profound changes under his leadership. With our worship of change, radical change, we have tended to lend to the word "innovate" all kinds of positive connotations, but change is not always good and is far from always positive. The Technocrat triumphs, in part, because he justifies his actions in the name of change and innovation, and we worship at the feet of these idols.

139

2) The manager is a copy, the leader, an original.
Message? Being an original is good (read, Artist), being a copy is bad (read, Technocrat). It is true, as we saw above, that the Technocrat loves to copy and that the Artist abhors it. But what about the Craftsman? He is a bit of both. He works within traditions (copies) and innovates, experiments, risks at the margin (original). If we give vent to our animosity toward copying, we throw the Craftsman out with the bathwater.

3) The manager maintains; the leader develops.
I don't think so. The Craftsman maintains *and* develops. The Artist develops while he lets the Craftsman maintain, and the Technocrat *undermines* maintenance and *pretends* to develop. When we condemn maintenance, in principle, and exalt development, we willy-nilly add fuel to the Technocrat's bonfire on which he roasts the Artist and the Craftsman.

4) The manager focuses on systems and structure, the leader on people.
The Technocrat certainly focuses on systems and structures. No complaint there. But the Artist? Does he focus on people? Not really. Basically he's a very private, even solitary person, or at least oscillates between gregariousness and solitariness depending on his mood. He likes people, but his *focus is outside* the organization, on dreams and deals. It's the Craftsman who focuses on people, his people. He looks at the task and matches it to the people. If he doesn't have someone to do the task, he trains one of his trusted people to do it. He invests his time and the organization's money in someone. He prefers to invest in an existing employee who already understands the business, because he believes that understanding the business is just as important as knowing how to accomplish the task. In fact, he believes that the two — knowing and understanding — are inseparable. Remember, we learned earlier from Polanyi that craftsmanship in general comes from this distinction between knowing and understanding. The craft of singing, for example, is "the science of acoustics *joined* to an experiential understanding of the

body" (emphasis is mine). Try to imagine using just words — no singing — to teach someone who has no idea what singing is, how to sing: "Well, ah, you open your mouth and you push air out through your lungs . . . "

5) The manager relies on control; the leader inspires trust.

Yes and no. The Technocrat certainly relies on control. He has to. He's scared. And the Artist certainly inspires excitement, but does he really inspire trust? Certainly he needs it. He needs trust desperately in order to have the time to complete his design. But does he inspire trust in the whole of the organization? Sometimes. More often, however, he inspires trust among the Craftsmen in his immediate entourage; he's not in the habit of interacting much with people beyond his entourage. He's too busy dreaming and creating. It's the Craftsmen who inspire trust in the rest of the organization. It's the Craftsmen who engender loyalty ("He really went out on a limb to defend me and didn't even tell them that it was my fault!") and trust ("Tomorrow will be largely the same as today. I won't be fired on a whim or arbitrarily because the whiz kids are 'reengineering'") and dedication ("He really believes in what we're doing; I'm proud to be a banker and to work with him") and self-confidence ("He let me cut my teeth on that project. He trusted me. I guess I'm competent") and humility ("Boy, I thought I had a brilliant idea, but he showed me why it wouldn't work. Oh, well, back to the drawing board").

6) The manager has a short-range view, the leader, long-range.

Again, yes and no. The Technocrat certainly has a short-range view and is preoccupied by today's results. But with the help of futurism, he who once had only illusions of control now has the vocabulary of vision and the language of dreams. And he also has long-range plans that consist of a trend-line extrapolation into the future of his short-term successes. If you see his plans, you might think he has a long-range view, but he doesn't. The script reads something like, "Today, we have eliminated thirty percent of our inefficiencies (read, people) and we have achieved a return on investment of ten percent; next year we will have eliminated fifty percent of our inefficiencies and will achieve a return on investment of twelve percent, and by 1995, fifteen percent." Except that, as a Craftsman pointed out, "By 1995 we'll be dead." And they were.

There's no doubt that the Artist has a long-range perspective; so long that he sometimes loses sight of today, or of how to get from today to tomorrow. That's where the Craftsman's medium-term vision comes in and is indispensable. Remember? The Craftsman is the guy who builds the bridges. James, Mike and Cobb would never try to pretend that they could have built what they did without the able Craftsmen on whom they relied.

7) The manager asks how and when, the leader, what and why.
Both the Craftsman and the Technocrat ask how and when. Both the Craftsman and the Artist ask what and why. The Craftsman asks why when the Technocrat proposes a new theoretical idea to fix something that isn't broken.

8) The manager has his eye on the bottom line, the leader, on the horizon.
The Technocrat and the Craftsman and the Artist all watch the bottom line. The Technocrat watches it for his glory, to show off, to show the world he's a great administrator. The Artist watches it as a guide to the correctness of his long-term vision, to make sure he's picked the right things to do. The Craftsman watches it carefully to *protect* the future. He knows that if the bottom line is in trouble, the institution and its people will be in trouble. And yes, it's true that the Artist has his eye on the horizon, but it's the Craftsman who sees the hills and gullies that have to be crossed to get there.

9) The manager imitates; the leader originates.
This is basically the same as the difference between a copy and an original in point number (2).

10) The manager accepts the status quo; the leader challenges it.
Not entirely. The Artist certainly challenges the status quo in terms
of his vision. But the Technocrat challenges the status quo with
respect to the organization of work — constantly. There are new people and new organization charts all the time. One Craftsman told us,
"They seemed to be fascinated with tinkering with the thing. You
know. Systems and structures." The Craftsman *respects* the status quo;
he doesn't believe that everything we did in the past is necessarily bad
or everything about the future is necessarily good. His motto is
"Change if necessary but not necessarily change." The more we give
credence to the notion that change is always an unqualified good
thing, the more we undermine the Craftsman.

11) The manager is the classic good soldier; the leader, his own person.
The Artist is certainly his own person, but if anything, the Craftsman
is the classic good soldier: loyal, dedicated, respectful of hierarchy and
chain of command. The Technocrat is loyal to nobody but himself.
Not to his boss, not to his organization, not even to his industry. He'll
jump ship if it will promote his own interests and he'll stab his own
mother in the back if she gets in his way. The Craftsman is also his own
person; principled and honourable, he is not easily swayed or seduced.

**12) The manager does things right; the leader, the right thing.
The Craftsman does both.**

I hope I've made plain the nature of the problem. If reality consisted
of only two types of people — the leader and the manager, or my Artist
and my Technocrat — then who would have difficulty with choice?
Not me. I'll take the leader any day of the week. But if I do, I must be
prepared to make certain sacrifices, such as doing things right (12),
ignoring systems and structures (4), control (5), the medium-term (6),
the bottom line (8) and so on, sacrifices I am not prepared to make. In
addition, I'll lose mentoring, a certain stability and continuity that is

necessary for most mortals, organizational "glue" that comes from loyalty and dedication and, in general, leadership that is characterized by realism and conviction, if not by vision. When we imagine a world polarized into these two camps, the manager and the leader, we lose the man in the middle. He becomes invisible. We long for Artists, but they are rare birds. In their stead, we get wolves in sheep's clothing — the Technocrats who, with their *beau discours* (beautiful talk), imitate Artists and Craftsmen. We make their con job easy by worshipping at the golden calves of Expertise and Change.

Why have I had to devote so much time to someone else's ideas about leadership? Well, because of that Collingwood quotation with which I began this chapter. You have to spend time on *good* theories, not stupid ones. From good theories, if you are not indolent, you can learn something. Secondly, everybody follows the *best*. Hervé Sérieyx, a French management consultant, has much the same things as Bennis to say about leadership. So do all the minor, and not-so-minor, leadership consultants floating around hawking their wares: "You, too, can be a visionary leader. Just take five minutes and fill out this application form for my seminar." This leadership thing is the talk of the town, and I'm afraid the cure has become, if not worse than the disease, just as bad.

Obviously I sympathize with, and share to a large extent, the frustration we've all felt about Technocrats, or managers, if you prefer. (I no longer like this distinction between leaders and managers, because I prefer to say simply that there are good managers and bad managers.) Like everyone else, I'm sick to death of their pretensions and their sermonettes. I yearn for new inspirations. We want to get rid of the Technocrats and their inhuman, and inhumane, logic and bring back passion and creativity and imagination and experimentation. So, we have had to denounce them and show how wrongheaded they've been to imagine that life could be so easily controlled and planned and people turned into robots. But in order to undermine them, we are driven to an opposite extreme; we want passion and *not* logic, miracles and oracles and *not* plans and realism. But these are babies that I don't want to throw out with the bathwater.

Furthermore, as much as I love Artists — James and Mike and Cobb are delightful people — there is neither a need for Artists everywhere and at all times, nor enough of them to go around. In my organization, there were four at the top in the space of sixty years! Artists have always been a distinct minority, usually marginalized, most often denigrated. True visionaries are usually broke; that's what being a visionary means. No one believes you. Nostradamus wasn't called a visionary until people found some of his predictions in his grave. Jesus Christ was crucified. Galileo was put on trial. So was Socrates. As George Bernard Shaw said, "All great truths begin as blasphemies." If your favourite futurist is rich, take him with a grain of sceptical salt.

Finally, what are we going to do with all the rest of the people? The vast majority of whom are Craftsmen? Two stories to illustrate what I mean.

#1. A young man, a twenty-eight-year-old MBA student of ours, came into my office the other day. Here is the gist of our conversation.

> *Student:* I was talking with professors X and Y and they sent me to you because you teach leadership. What I want to know is, what is it, this leadership thing?
>
> *Me:* Why?
>
> *Student:* Well, I've been working for [a major telecommunications company] full-time and now part-time, while I do my MBA, for the last eight years, and every time I come up for evaluation, I don't do well in this leadership category. I ask them what they mean by it and no one can tell me what it is. I thought maybe you could tell me.

Well, what they mean is this: Are you inspiring, imaginative, visionary, creative, intuitive? I gave him a copy of Bennis's book. What I didn't tell him, what I didn't have the heart to tell him, is that hell will freeze over before he'll become a leader by this definition. He's intelligent

145

and capable, eager to learn and to contribute, calm and collected, sincere and honest, but we don't value what he has to offer.

#2. A young woman, twenty-three, can't get a job. She has an advanced degree in management, is bright, attractive and trilingual — French, English and Spanish. She's good with numbers and with people. But she goes into an interview and some jerk inevitably asks her if she's a "leader." She's honest, so she says, "Well, sometimes. I mean . . . I mean, it depends. It depends on the circumstances." This is not what the interviewer wants to hear. He wants to hear, "You bet. I was the captain of this and that team. I got the best marks in school. All my friends look to me to tell them what to do. I'm very intuitive. I've been looking at your business and what you need is . . ." Confidence, right? Ideas, right? Imagination, right? Modesty? Nope. Experience? Nope. Narcissism? Yep. Guess who replies this way in a job interview? A budding Technocrat. So, these interviewers who are looking for exciting young Artists are getting, for the most part, impressive, "brilliant" little Technocrats.

These kinds of interviews are going on all over the world at all levels of our organizations. Especially at the top. Let's listen in on an imaginary set of interviews with an Artist, a Craftsman and a Technocrat.

> *Interviewer:* So what would you do if you get the top job?
> *Artist:* I don't really know. We'll have to see. I have a few ideas, but they're sort of vague right now. I guess you'll just have to trust me. [Remember what Cobb said? "It's clear but fluid. Action brings precision. Very vague but becomes clear in the act of transformation. Creation is the storm."]
> *Craftsman:* Well, we have to build on our strengths. I've been working here for the last twenty-five years and it's clear to me that whenever we've got off track with what we know best, we get in trouble. I think the widgets division has lost steam because the manager there

doesn't know what a widget is. There have been so many changes that the sales staff is demoralized. There are no really big things that need to be done, just a lot of relatively minor things, experiments that will add up.

Technocrat: Now, I don't know anything about your business in particular, but all businesses have to decentralize, cut costs, empower people, emphasize quality, get into strategic alliances, become fleet-footed, supple, flexible, able to turn on a dime because the communications revolution is overtaking us, revolutionizing, globalizing everything almost overnight. Everybody is going to be a knowledge-worker operating out of his house or his car but linked into networks. The organization as we know it is going to disappear.

Who do you think gets the job? Who would you pick? The Artist is far too vague; he's a trend-setter not a trend-follower. He's a maker, a doer, not a talker; like Isadora Duncan, who cried "If I could say it, I wouldn't have to dance it," or Robert Motherwell, "All my life I've been working on the work — every canvas a sentence or paragraph of it." Since everything the Technocrat answers has become conventional wisdom, the Artist will be the last to employ it. He hates conventional wisdom.

The Craftsman is far too dull and we're in a hurry.

The Technocrat mentions all the new management tools, but what he says is essentially vacuous. It would be like your contractor saying, "Well, I'm going to use screwdrivers and saws, and hammers and nails to build your house." You reply, "Yes, but what's it going to look like?" The Technocrat talks the talk. "He multiplieth words without understanding."[3] He seems imaginative. He seems farsighted. He reads the futurist magazines with their trend-line predictions. He sounds good. He high-jacks the language of vision, but of course he won't decentralize or empower. He doesn't give a hoot about quality; he doesn't even know what you produce. Technocrats are the ones who read the management literature and go to the conferences, because they want to be on top of the vocabulary and they like conventional wisdom. In an earlier era, they were the ones who promoted the recipes of matrix management, management by objectives, synergy, and now, with the able assistance of institutionalized crystal-ball gazers and the pseudoscience of futurism, they masquerade as visionary leaders. They get the jobs. And that, ladies and gentlemen, makes me mad. And that's why I say, the leadership cure is getting worse than the technocratic disease.

Neither Abraham Zaleznik nor Warren Bennis intended for this to happen. Both of them want real Artists, real leaders, not imitators. But you cannot control what others will do with your work, nor can you control the climate of opinion in which it will be received. Zaleznik and Bennis are not responsible for futurism's hold on us. And while Bennis seems ambivalent about it (note "becoming" in the title of his book *On Becoming a Leader*), I feel safe in saying that Zaleznik certainly doesn't believe that anyone can *learn* to be a visionary leader, lateral thinking notwithstanding. But because we have polarized the world into two camps, the bad guys (managers) and the good guys (leaders), and because we have popularized the idea that anybody can *become* a good guy with enough training or desire, we have unwittingly lent the Technocrat more ammunition to drive out the Craftsman and the genuine Artist.

Craftsmen represent the vast majority of people, young or old. So I ask again, what are we going to do with all the people if we only now value Artists, or what Sérieyx calls *l'acteur/auteur* (actor/author), at all levels of the organization?

> Wanted: volatile, emotional, unpredictable, imaginative, self-starter.
> All others need not apply.

Oh, you say you don't want emotional, volatile and unpredictable, just imaginative? Sorry, they only come in a package: character. I can offer you a dedicated, loyal, honest, realistic, knowledgeable package, but the imagination bit will be rather limited; do you really need a lot of imagination or will a little do?

Collingwood told us, at the beginning of this chapter, that the upshot of examining good theories can "always be expressed in some form as this: 'The Theory is untenable as regards its general conclusions; but it has established certain points which must henceforth be taken into account.'" In my view, the theories we have seen here are "untenable as regards their general conclusions." Let's turn now to a discussion of "certain points which must henceforth be taken into account" when we're thinking about what organizations might really need.

What we've learned from Zaleznik and Bennis, and what must henceforth be taken into account, is what we *don't* want, what leadership *isn't*. We don't want rigidity. We don't want an exclusive preoccupation with today at the expense of tomorrow. We don't want people to be treated like robots. We don't want to suffocate in systems and rules.

We want vibrant, interesting organizations. We want organizations with enough flexibility to adapt to an as yet unknown, and I claim unknowable, future. But those organizations also have to be stable enough to provide us ordinary people with a sense of continuity without which we feel lost. We want experimentation. But we also want the tried and true. We want long-range perspective, but not at the expense of losing contact with the present and the immediate future. We need both to respect and to challenge the status quo by going back and by going forward. We need to do the right thing and to do things right. We want and need true visionaries who discover new paths, but we can't expect them to make all our struggles disappear. They are not our saviours. We need to take charge of our own fates, to accept responsibility. And finally we need very badly to be able to recognize charlatans, con men and false prophets, and we need to stop bowing down before the golden calf of Expertise, which pretends to combine Competence and Virtue.[4]

In Chapter Ten we're going to examine what organizations need. It ends with the only recipe you'll find in this book: how to recognize a Technocrat. In Chapter Eleven we'll see how education may help to minimize their numbers, or at least to keep them in their place.

Ten What Do Organizations Need?

Yet it was observed that these mechanistic explanations always left Hamlet out of their play; that, in brief, like all merely mechanistic explanations, they left out the vital spark or soul or essence — the essential mark or quality or character that made the phenomenon what it was. . . . Whatever well-formulated and even demonstrable "truth" these scientific explanations had, they had obviously no "reality" nor any profound relation to the living experience of any man. . . . They told us many interesting superficial things. They never uttered the secret.

LUDWIG LEWISOHN[1]

Although we hear a lot of talk these days about something called the Learning Organization, organizations don't learn and they don't see and they don't do anything. "Organization" is a concept, a shorthand; it is the name we give to a certain collectivity of people. It is a useful way to be able to talk about these collectivities without having to say every time, "Such and such a group of people organized by some principle to attain some objective or other." It is a useful *abstraction*, for some purposes but not for all. Abstractions, concepts, neither learn nor see; people do. North American business has been accused, for example, of taking a short-term view at the expense of the long-term. Is this, strictly speaking, true? I don't think so. North American business is an abstraction; it doesn't exist. It doesn't take long *or* short views. North American businessmen are *real*. If North American business has taken a short-term view it is because North American business*men* have taken a short-term view. And by now it's clear, I hope, that not *all* North American businessmen take a short-term view. The Artist usually doesn't. The Craftsman usually doesn't. The Technocrat does, and we have given him free rein. That's not his fault. It's ours. So let's own up to our part in his triumph. We should have known better, but we didn't. No point crying over spilt milk. What we can do about it now is what matters.

Since organizations are composed of people, it seems to me not farfetched to imagine that what may apply to people in general may apply equally to organizations as a whole. Since every organization faces its own unique challenge, there are precious few things they all need, very few universals. Just basic things: a team of people working together to promote the three E's, Efficacy, Expertise and Efficiency.

E FFICACY: ON DOING THE RIGHT THING

Efficacy is, to paraphrase Peter Drucker, the dean of American business commentators, doing the right thing. Efficacy is making the right choices about goals. How do organizations go about setting goals or strategies? There have been, essentially, two dominant schools of thought about creating organizational mission: the rational/analytic and the experiential. The rational/analytic view insists that you determine an appropriate strategy by collecting a lot of information about your markets, your competitors and your suppliers and you, in effect, *calculate* your strategy. You develop a *plan.* This notion of strategy as plan is, of course, an old and creditable one. Plans are good. However, in the realm of human activity, it's tough to plan. The planning mode is based on the assumption that the future will mimic the past. This is so because analysis always comes late to the party; it is based on collecting historical "facts," what used to be, and extrapolating (projecting trend-lines) those facts into the future. One problem with this approach is that the facts need interpretation and only the Technocrat thinks that the "facts speak for themselves." A second problem is that change is unfathomable, and trend-line extrapolations are seldom accurate (haven't we been given trend-line projections that purport to prove again and again, year after year, that our governments' deficits are going to disappear by 1992, 1993, 1995, 1997, 2000?). At one time they told us that you couldn't have inflation and unemployment at the same time (the Phillips curve), but we learned the hard way that that particular trend didn't sustain itself.

What if everything defies the trends? As Cobb told us, things always change, "government, death, technology." In 1986 Cobb tried to explain to me a complicated set of financial manoeuvres that would allow his company to swallow an organization twice its size; I didn't understand a word he said except the name of the target company. *Five years later* I sat in a meeting and listened to his successor talk about the results of a planning exercise — for which he had paid a consultant $400,000. The analysis came up with the same target company as Cobb had! Trouble is, it was five years too late. Everything had changed. The trends were not borne out. The group had no money and the window of opportunity had closed. So, it's not that analysis is bad; it's that it's slow. It does not lend itself very well to prediction, to determining long-range goals.

Frustrated with what was seen as this lack of realism in the rational/analytic, blueprint model of strategy-making, management scholars like Henry Mintzberg and James Brian Quinn turned to a more experiential model. Quinn told us that, in the real world, strategy does not "spring full-blown like Minerva from the brow of Jupiter," because it "involves forces of such great number, strength and combinatory powers that one cannot predict events in any probabilistic sense. Hence, *logic* dictates that one proceed flexibly and experimentally"[2] (emphasis is mine). He called what we needed "logical incrementalism." Mintzberg would add his eloquent voice to this in his award-winning Harvard Business Review article "Crafting

Strategy." And Tom Peters would reach fame and fortune by cele-brating experimenting, acting, trying things. On the other side of the Atlantic, Hervé Sérieyx would argue that strategy is out and tactics are in.[3] Quinn hinted at the assumptions behind this glorification of experimentation. We cannot predict the future. We are like the blind. We cannot see through the dense fog of turbulence and complexity. We must use a blind man's cane to tap on objects around us.

Well, all right, I can't see through the fog, but some people can. Artists can. To make en*light*ened choices (note my emphasis on "light"), we need to be able to see. We need vision. Now, because we have seemed as a society to have lost our way, we cry out for vision and for visionary leaders as though such people could provide miraculous answers for us. This is, I think, the reason for the dramatically increased interest in charismatic leadership and for the Technocrat's success in passing himself off as visionary. But this enthusiasm, although perfectly understandable, is misplaced.

What is vision anyway? If we all walked around with binoculars affixed to our eyes, would life be better? We would see farther, you say. Yes, but we would stumble on the underbrush of life. Myopic peo-ple are obliged to use glasses to see, let us say, mid-range objects. I remember, at age six, trying on my best friend's glasses and exclaim-ing, "I didn't know you were supposed to be able to see the leaves on the trees!" To myopic me, the trees were just big green balls. But, if farsighted people use my glasses, they can't see anything clearly; they lose their mid-range sight. If I use reading glasses, I lose my short-range sight. And so on and so on. What's the point of this seemingly pointless digression? Well, the fact is, we, and organizations, need all kinds of vision — short, medium and long range.

Will it come as any surprise if I say that all organizations need Artists at some point in time, at the top or in some specific function like R&D or marketing or finance? Artists are the ones with the binoculars. If you can get your hands on a real one, so much the bet-ter. But your odds are about one in a hundred, and Artists are tough to recognize. By their deeds are they known, not by their talk. Of course we need visionary leaders, but there's some truth, too, in the Craftsman's comment that "He [Cobb] never implemented the head-office systems that would have allowed the decentralized management of the subsidiaries. So, the wheels started falling off all the carts." Wheels tend to fall off carts if you don't pay attention to them from time to time. The Artist has a tendency to ignore the details. It's not that he's not analytical — he is; James and Cobb could perform, on a scrap of paper, imaginative financial contortions that would make your head swim. But don't ask him to work out all the minutiae. He's not interested in the details. He gets impatient with them. That's why he delegates so easily: "Here. Here's the outline. Run with it. I have to see so and so, go here, go there." Details bore him. That's one of the reasons he surrounds himself with Craftsmen and Technocrats.

The Craftsman, on the other hand, responds to the Artist's visions with things like, "Okay. I like it but you can't get there from here. It's too great a leap. We will have to do such and such by 1997 if you want to get there by 2000." He's practical, realistic. Rome can't be built in a day. Systems and people can't be changed overnight; one told us, "It takes time to weld a team together and to solve human problems. They're not machines that you can just turn on and off." Most people need stability more than they need, or can handle, change; you know, like those stress scales that tell you that if you've changed jobs, cities, spouses, whether happily or not, your stress level is likely to be very high. Change, good or bad, is stressful and disorienting. The Craftsman knows and respects this. He's wise and realistic, and his vision is medium-range.

There's another kind of vision for which we have expressions like, "He went over it with a fine-tooth comb," meaning, he examined it in great detail. We want our lawyers, for example, to examine contracts very carefully. We get them to read the fine print. We're not happy at all if they say things like, "It looks good to me," in a cavalier way. I don't know about you, but I want my airline pilot to look very carefully at all the gauges and dials in front of him before we take off. So, more generally, we need a kind of microscopic vision too. Guess who's good at microscopic vision? Yep. The Technocrat. He'll tell you, gladly, all the things you're doing wrong, all the short-range weaknesses in the system that may impede, or even render impossible, the accomplishment of medium- and long-term goals. This is necessary; as Benjamin Franklin reminded us, "A little neglect can breed mischief . . . for want of a nail, the shoe was lost; for want of a shoe the horse was lost; and for want of a horse the rider was lost." Then, although the general had a great strategy, he lost the battle. The trick is to keep this short-range view in its place and under control. I don't want to throw "brilliant" out. I want it working for me. I want it subservient to "humane" and "realistic." The Technocrat is great at managing things; I just don't want him to have any authority over people or dreams.

Does this mean we can dispense with experimentation and with planning if we have vision, if we have Artists? Or dispense with vision if we have experimentation? Or dispense with plans and control if we have both? I don't think so. You see, these theories are not wrong; they simply try to do too much, to cover too much ground, to be all things to all people, to all times and to all organizations. They leave out context, particular tasks, particular times, particular organizations.

The "planning mode" is right for organizations that already know their mission, not for finding it. I read recently that it takes General Motors eight hours more to assemble a car that it does Ford.[4] It seems pretty clear to me that GM needs a plan. It may also need a vision and a sense of experimentation, but that's another matter.

The experimental mode is right for organizations to adapt their mission to day-to-day, month-to-month realities. There's a great deal of experimentation going on these days in the financial-services industry as people jockey for position and as consumer needs change with the bulging, now middle-aged baby boomers. Does that mean that financial institutions don't need a plan or a dream? I don't think so.

The visionary mode is necessary for organizations that have lost their way, but it is false to say that all our organizations and institutions have lost their way. (Chairman Mao believed in permanent revolution and look what it produced.) James's initial vision sustained an organization for at least twenty years. Who knows? The two other Artists, Mike and Cobb, might have sustained it for the next twenty years had they been given time. But no, we pull the rug out from under them as soon as they seem to falter. We get scared. Anyway, the visionary mode might be necessary in certain functions at certain times. For example, it might be good in marketing, in R&D and even in finance; creative financing has allowed many a company to pursue its long-range dreams. In governments, it seems to me we need some vision right now in the policy-planning apparati, but not necessarily at the top at all times. *It depends.*

Finally, these theories about organizational mission are incomplete, because they leave out character and its influence on judgement. With what we now know about the Artist, the Craftsman and the Technocrat, which mode do you think each will prefer? Don't you think that the Technocrat, with his need for security and order, will operate by plan and defend to the death that this plan is absolutely the only way to go? Experiments sometimes fail and we know how he feels about "mistakes" and we know how his employees work to rule to avoid making mistakes, like the Craftsman who told me, "I'm trying to turn myself into a robot, but it's not working very well." And, we know how the Technocrat feels about vision; he thinks visionaries are dreamers, confused, not serious. They don't keep their noses to the grindstone. Is it any wonder, then, that the idea of strategic planning held sway in the past twenty years since it was so well suited to the technocratic mentality that had triumphed?

And the Artist. How do you think he feels about plans? He told us how: "That stuff's just an excuse not to work. All they do is produce tons of paper that just goes into a shredder eventually anyway, so what's the point?" And the Craftsman adds, "I just keep my head down and look after business." He doesn't like plans either. For him, plans are unreal. He likes experimentation. He likes trial and error, taking small risks. He likes getting better and better at what he already knows how to do. He'll use his old tool first, but try a new tool to see if it performs better on an exotic piece of wood with which he's unfamiliar. He'll seek advice from someone who's already worked with it; he keeps his ear to the ground for information.

So, I conclude, these theories are not, I repeat, wrong. They seem to advocate mutually exclusive options — planning, experimenting, imagining — which are not mutually exclusive but which depend heavily on the context, on the task, and on who is in the driver's seat. Efficacy, doing the right thing, means doing the right things today, next week and next year. So, I claim, organizations need all sorts of vision, short-, medium- and long-term. One is not a substitute for the other. The trick is to have the right people in the right place at the right time and to make sure that the Technocrat has loads of influence and not a shred of power.

EXPERTISE: ON GETTING BETTER AND BETTER AT WHAT WE DO

How do we acquire expertise? With experience, with learning. The Learning Organization has become a new catchphrase, but as I've tried to argue, organizations don't learn, people do. So let's look first at how people learn and then ask ourselves what that means for organizations.

I claim that there are essentially three ways in which people, and humanity (which is just people writ large), learn. Santayana told us, "Man's progress has a poetic phase in which he imagines a world." The poetic phase, or if you like the poetic *way* of learning, is discontinuous. It breaks radically with the standard way of viewing things. It unlearns in order to learn — "A painting moves forward by a series of destructions; what would live in song immortally, must in life first perish." This form of learning is deeply personal; it stems from the peculiar vision of an individual. It is not a collective enterprise. Culturally, we have always relied on our visionaries to lead the way. In science, we call the visionary a "genius," like Einstein; in letters, a "poet," like T. S. Eliot; in politics, a "statesman," like Churchill; in business, a "leader"; generically, an "Artist." But the Artist, far from ignoring the past, must possess it in order to break with it. The imaginative leap comes to the prepared mind (like Copernicus or Einstein), and the unprepared mind, without experience, is just an amateur, a dabbler.

Then there is continuous learning. The new insight offered by an individual genius is transformed into a collective enterprise. We take the insight, which is usually fragmentary and vague, and we worry away at it. We work out the bugs. We put flesh on the skeleton. The essential method of this continuous learning is trial and error; you work on my error with another trial. We try to articulate, to make clear and concrete, the new insight. Kuhn calls this "normal science" in the domain of science, but it is true in all domains. James's insight, his dream, his metaphor, was sculpted, shaped, made concrete by the skilled Craftsmen he trusted and to whom he granted authority. Without experience, without knowledge of the past — what has worked and what hasn't — there is no learning.

Finally there is a third form of learning, and it requires neither imagination nor practice to make it our own. It requires diligence and concentration, not skill or imagination. It is called reading, studying, analysing, examining, other people's work. It, too, is largely an individual endeavour and not a collective one. We call someone who performs this well knowledgeable; if, after a great deal of analytic (not life) experience and diligence, he performs it very well, we call him brilliant.

So experience is essential to imagination, to skill and to brilliance, to all three forms of learning. I see this every day in a classroom. In any given group of thirty or forty students, there are always a couple who don't need me; their insights are stronger and more peculiar than my own — Artists. There are always two or three who are neither diligent nor imaginative nor skilled and cannot (or will not) learn — fools. And there are always one or two who claim to know everything already — "It says on page 24 that that's how you do it" — Technocrats. Then there is the great majority, varying in native intelligence to be sure, but all capable and willing to learn collectively, from each other and from teachers like me — Craftsmen. The case method of teaching, experiential learning, is perfect for this group. They learn skills. Some pretend that only experiential learning is good but, of course, this is another piece of narcissism. We need also to learn from books, from magnificent lecturers and from the sudden inspirations of vision.

So, in an organizational context, we need people who have different ways of learning. The North American auto industry, it's alleged, foundered on the rocks of Japanese quality. We hear talk about creating higher quality. Well, where does quality come from? It depends. Can't it come from paying meticulous attention to detail? Can't it come from diligence? Producing an automobile, for example, requires producing a large array of parts, each one perfect. You don't want to receive your new car and have the handles fall off the doors — "Oops. Sorry. We missed that one."

Can't it, doesn't it, also come from trial and error, from experience? How can you know that something new will work if you don't know what has already been tried? Aren't all the automobile companies learning from one another, copying one another and making marginal improvements on one another?

Of course, we also learn from fundamental innovation, which reshapes the way we look at the world. Like the way the Mustang reshaped a segment of the market. Like the way Macintosh reshaped the image of the computer. All the studies of major innovation show that it comes largely from individuals, not from groups or from large organizations. For that we need inventors.

Will it come as any surprise, then, if I say that organizations need all kinds of people who learn in different ways?

EFFICIENCY: ON CONTROL

Since Fayol's day in the early part of this century, how to organize to accomplish tasks efficiently, with the least amount of effort, has been a serious preoccupation in management. Until, I suppose, the sixties, efficient organizing was seen to be pretty straightforward and was based, essentially, on "span of control." People quibbled over whether one ought to have five, six, seven or eight people reporting to any one manager, but few quarrelled with the idea of span of control as a basic organizing principle. Span of control, of course, presupposes authority and hierarchy, and as of at least the sixties, both of these principles have been undermined. Early on, they were contested by things such as "matrix management" (read, many different bosses), later by "self-organizing organizations" (whatever that means), but most frequently by something more general called "participative management." Now, participative management means many different things to many different people; there is no single definition nor one all-important author or book on which we can rely. It's sort of just floating in the air — which makes me suspect it may be rather light.

Who could be (publicly) against participation? I think the participative-management impulse represents an intelligent, normal reaction against authoritarianism. It's a reaction against the idea that grown people should be treated like children and told what to do. In fact, we are no longer even allowed to treat children like children, so I guess it stands to reason we shouldn't treat adults like children. Or does it? We have been told that authority structures stamp out creativity in both adults and children; that organizations need the creativity of all their members and that, therefore, authority structures are bad, bad, bad. But are they?

No one likes authoritarianism, but authoritarianism, as my friend and colleague Laurent Lapierre has reminded me, is not the same thing as authority.[5] Authority has to do with setting boundaries and limits. As New York Mayor Rudolph Giuliani stressed in a recent speech, freedom is about authority: "We see only the oppressive side of authority . . . [but] freedom is about the willingness of every single human being to cede to lawful authority a great deal of discretion about what you do."[6] Great art, too, depends vitally on limits; if there are no limits to transcend, no traditions to fight, you don't get Artists, you get amateurs; necessity is the mother of invention. Limits are the reality principle in operation; the schizophrenic who produces paintings creates images that are interesting but meaningless.[7] The parent of every adolescent knows the importance of limits; adolescent psychiatrists tell us the limits have to be there so that the child can define himself or herself *against* them. No limits, no identity. It's tough, and tougher and tougher all the time, to define such limits, but it must be done. (In parenthesis, British child psychiatrist D. W. Winnicott says that the task of every parent of an adolescent is survival — just survival.)

There are some emergency situations, like war, that require strong authority. Let's listen in on a hypothetical conversation in the World War I trenches:

> *Captain:* "So men, I thought we might go up into no man's land tonight. What do you think?"
> *Soldiers:* "Gee, I dunno captain, it's pretty bright tonight and . . ."

Sometimes authority is indispensable.

Ah, but that's a false analogy, you say. You can't compare organizations to war. Okay, how about this? We once hired a gold-medal-winning MBA graduate to work for us. The person was relatively experienced and very bright. We hired her to develop a new aspect of our business. I told her, "Here it is. Here are the basic parameters. How it gets done is up to you." Every week or so I asked her how things were coming and she told me that she was "writing up a plan."

161

Good, I thought. We've finally got someone serious around here. Someone who knows what she's doing. (In those days, I was very impressed by plans.) Well, time wore on, and on, and on. People began to suggest to me, not very subtly, that she should be fired. Finally in exasperation I asked her what was wrong. She replied, in equal exasperation, that she didn't know what I wanted and so she couldn't *do* a plan. Some people, no matter how bright or well trained they are, can't fill vacuums; they need direction, and I'd been doing her no favour at all to ask her to work autonomously. She was miserable. It made her feel totally, but totally, inadequate. This was not kindness, it was inhumane. I gave her a few more details — the few I possessed — and afterward she performed beautifully and, sometimes, creatively.

Take another example. Suppose we are in a regime of participative management interpreted as management by consensus. We have four people who are bright and creative and hardworking, and one lazy son of a gun who contests everything everyone else wants to do and has a right to be heard. Doesn't listening to him constantly just demoralize everyone else? Is participative management letting everyone have equal airtime?

Take another example. Between the two great wars, people wanted to play. In England, everyone thought that the country's military preparedness was perfectly adequate. Churchill disagreed, and it was Churchill and not the majority who was right. Does participative management mean rule by the majority? Does it make leadership unnecessary? Will someone please clarify this for me? Does it just mean listening?

If, to take the best-case scenario, it means listening, who is good at it? Does the Artist listen? Well, yes he does, if you can catch him between airplanes. Does the Technocrat listen? Nope. If you're looking forward to participative management as listening, you're in for a big disappointment with him — although he talks a lot about listening when masquerading as a Craftsman. Who listens attentively all the time? You got it. It's the Craftsman. Does he abdicate authority? Never. Does he take responsibility? Always — even if the bad idea came from one of his apprentices.

I look at this participation thing in the following way:

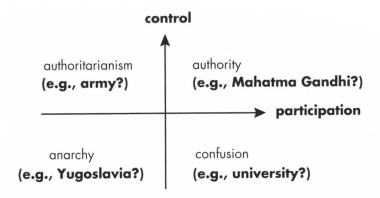

control

authoritarianism
(e.g., army?)

authority
(e.g., Mahatma Gandhi?)

participation

anarchy
(e.g., Yugoslavia?)

confusion
(e.g., university?)

It depends. It depends on what you want to accomplish and how urgently. In the university, for example, change takes a very, very long time and is hideously inefficient by design. We wish to preserve the value of participation, we seek consensus, and academics don't willingly give up control. Society as a whole gets very frustrated by our inability to respond instantly to its desires. (I, for one, don't think universities should respond quickly to society's whims. That's not our job.)

The former Yugoslavia is a current example of anarchy, with no control and no formal, institutional, structured way for people to participate in the events that shape, and destroy, their lives. Anarchy is inefficient both because of an absence of control and because of an absence of structured participation.

The army, I submit, is the place for authoritarianism and strict chain of command and would be inefficient with more participation. So, I argue, would the cockpit of an airplane.

Pilot: "Joe, would you check the fuel gauge please."
Copilot: "It's not my job."

163

Pilot: "I've got my hands full here."

Passenger: "Would *someone* please check it!!"

In short, there's a continuous, delicate tension between the demands of control and the demands of participation. It can't be settled for all time, and not all organizations need more participative management. And I wonder where the urgency is, given that a recent survey conducted by a Quebec television program discovered that something like eighty percent of employees were satisfied with their immediate superiors because they were already being "listened to." Management is, I contend, a judicious and timely blend of control and participation. When control, when participation. I pick Gandhi as one of my heroes; he had a vision, and a sometimes domineering personal authority, but he also knew how and when to listen. You, no doubt, have your own example.

So in general, efficacy, experience and learning, and efficiency all depend on what you want to accomplish and who's doing the accomplishing. We have to reject all-purpose recipes. All-purpose flour is a great boon to ordinary cooks and I may win a local pie contest using it. I have no illusions, however, that I would win in a Parisian culinary contest. Most of us don't even want to enter such a contest.

Most of us, and most organizations, just have tasks to accomplish, which sometimes demand a lot of participation and sometimes a little, which sometimes demand a lot of authority (not authoritarianism) and sometimes a little, which sometimes demand a wholly new vision and sometimes just demand a lot of hard work. Some organizations do a lousy job of learning because they are packed, as our example was, only with diligence and not with imagination or with skill and experience. There were no new visions, because there were no Artists, just trend-line projections into an uncertain future. No experimentation, because there were no experimenters, no quality, because there was no *cult of excellence* — in short, no Craftsmen. People, not systems and recipes, make the difference.

How could we possibly have forgotten this? Because, for a variety of reasons, we have forgotten character. We are the slaves of some defunct philosophers. We have been taught that behaviour is everything: behaviourism. We have been taught that thinking is everything: man as information-processor. We have been taught that all men are created equal: egalitarianism. They are created *equal* in the sense that they deserve respect, but they are not created the *same*. These three things, and no doubt many more, have led us to imagine that anybody can be taught anything if given half a chance and the right method. We imagine that you can just lasso *acting* and reform behaviour with teaching; tell people how to be inspiring. Or you could just lasso *thinking* and teach people how to be visionary by thinking sideways or upside down. Or you could lasso *seeing* and teach people how their perception is distorted, so that there'll be no more, say, racism. But character doesn't work that way. It's a package. You can teach an Artist to watch for the details, but he can't walk the talk. You can teach a Technocrat the language of empowerment, but he can't walk the talk. You can teach the Craftsman the language of vision, but he can't walk the talk.

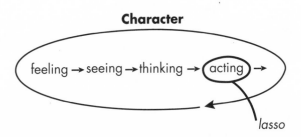

Here's an example of the distortion that our way of looking at people as information-processors has wrought. In Montreal, we recently had a group studying the problem of doctors sexually assaulting their patients. What do you think their solution was? Information. Resident doctors should be given more information. As if they don't know that such behaviour is immoral! The very few who transgress morality and ethical conduct don't need "information," they need punishment. For whatever twisted and distorted reasons of the human psyche, originating in feeling and passing through seeing and thinking and thence to an immoral act, we sometimes get psychopaths and sociopaths, and no amount of information can cure them. Therapy might, but some cases are notoriously resistant to therapy, notably, child molesters, psychopaths and sociopaths. People have to suffer before they will seek and use help, and these people do not suffer; they don't feel the pangs of conscience, guilt or remorse that would drive them to therapy. And they do not doubt, and doubt and suffering are the doors through which therapy can enter and be effective. Character is all of a piece. We need to recognize (re-cognize: to resume possession of, fifteenth century; to know again, sixteenth century) character. We need to be able to *see* the Artist and the Craftsman and the Technocrat, not as rigid categories, abstract concepts or boxes, but as central tendencies of individual human beings. While we would like to combine all three, we can't. Human beings aren't gods. Only gods combine all three. So, it turns out, Herbert Simon *was* wrong. Management always has been and always will be about the judicious selection of the right people for the right job and not primarily about training.

The first step in the resolution of any problem is its recognition. Here come the only recipes you will find in this book.

How Do You Recognize a Technocrat?

Technocrats come in all shapes and sizes and all guises. They are in all sectors — not just in private organizations, but in government, in non-profit associations, in politics, in movements as advocates of all sorts of different causes. You can't identify them by the causes they espouse, but only by the *way* they espouse them. We need to develop an instinctive capacity to recognize them. Recognition starts in *feeling* and proceeds to thought and judgement; as seventeenth-century French philosopher Blaise Pascal said, "The heart has its reasons which Reason does not know." I am now able to sense a Technocrat at fifty yards. I start to feel uncomfortable, slightly irritated, slightly suffocated, when I meet one. Gradually I'm able to put thoughts and names to my feelings. I hear a little sermonette from him and I know he thinks that everyone else is an imbecile, that only he possesses Truth, Justice and Morality.

He seems brilliant, but I sense rigidity. I know his mind is closed. I think we should start to develop a healthy suspicion of the description "brilliant." We used to have expressions that tried to capture this suspicion. We said, "Oh, him? He's *too clever by half*." The expression has fallen into disuse. "Too clever by half." What did that mean? It meant too clever, not for his own good, but for ours. We used to mistrust cleverness. "Oh, yes, he was a clever fellow," meaning, he was a fancy talker, too *clever* for us. "What a clever child!" meaning, ingenious and sometimes meaning, if you can't say something nice don't say anything at all; that is, the person wanted to say "what a brat" but found something nice to say instead. The earliest etymological origins of the word "clever" associate it with "claw."[8] That ought to tell us something! Brilliant and clever are both purely associated with the head; they tell us nothing about the heart, about imagination, about ethics. We should learn to say, "Brilliant, huh? That's nice. What else have you got?" And we should watch and listen for quite a while before we buy. We should become unrepentant doubting Thomases or, if you like, we should all "come from Missouri."

He's uncompromising and hardheaded. These two adjectives capture what I would put under the heading *disdain*, or disrespect. I think we need to develop antennae to detect disdain. The technocratic mentality is very sure of itself. Let's listen in on some hypothetical conversations:

Technocrat: "And so, in conclusion, the only crisis that matters right now is the ozone layer. We must shut down factory X."

A member of the audience: "I was just wondering what we will do with all the people who depend on that factory for their livelihood. And what about the town?"

Technocrat: "You've fallen for the same old line of reasoning. We can't worry about that; the facts show that the whole planet is at risk. The facts speak for themselves" (*you sentimental imbecile*).

Another context and another subject:

Technocrat: "And so, in conclusion, we have to ban smoking from the planet."

A member of the audience: "I was reading the other day in a medical journal that major depression and the propensity to cigarette smoking are highly correlated. These doctors were suggesting that we should be a bit careful with depressed people, because pushing them too hard to quit smoking may inadvertently push them into a major clinical depression."[9]

Technocrat: "The study was no doubt financed by the cigarette lobby [paranoid], and even if it's true, that's their problem [narcissistic]."

Another context and another subject:

Technocrat: "And so, in conclusion, we have to lay off 1436 people in the widgets division."

A member of the audience: "I was just wondering if we couldn't use some of those people to develop Edward's new product idea."

Technocrat: "Ed's new product idea will never see the light of day. Ed's a nice guy but he's a dreamer. Instant photography. Honestly. It doesn't make sense. It's not logical."

Now, the Technocrat might be right about the ozone layer, about smoking, about photography. Because he is brilliant, he often *is* right, but that's not the point. The point is that he's absolutely certain he's right; he's never wrong and other people are just too stupid to see it. The Technocrat never doubts, never gets depressed, always has an answer. Lucky him! Most of us live with a crushing sense of doubt. So, again, watch him. Does he ever waver? Does he ever question himself? Does he ever mock himself? Does his certitude ever falter?

I want to pick up on this depression bit. Psychiatrists tell us that depression is anger turned inward. In the simplest language possible, I think it's intimately connected with doubt. When we doubt our certitude, we have no enemy but ourselves for our lack of clarity. So we get mad at ourselves — depressed. As soon as we can find someone or something to blame *outside* ourselves, we can direct our anger outward and we're no longer depressed. The reason the Technocrat is never depressed is because he never doubts, and he never doubts because he *always* has someone or something to blame. The technocratic character is narcissistic: "There's nothing wrong with me; it's *them*. How dare they criticize me?" It's paranoid: "I'm nice, it's the *others* who are dangerous." It's compulsive: "I'm logical, *they're* emotional." They fulfil Oscar Wilde's definition of a cynic: Someone who knows the price of everything and the value of nothing. In short, beware of unflagging certitude in a messy world, and beware of anyone who just parrots conventional wisdom of whatever ilk, whatever political or social stripe.

HOW DO YOU RECOGNIZE AN ARTIST?

Unless his business is words, like a poet, you recognize an Artist by his deeds, not by his words. If he uses words, the words will surprise you; you won't have heard them before in quite the same way. He's unpredictable, remember? Just when you think you've got some subject truly mastered, he'll come along and push your head around, wake you up, make you question your certitudes. As soon as there is a bandwagon for something, he'll get off. He never brags; he doubts his own capacities. That's why James hired Cam.

How Do You Recognize a Craftsman?

Dead easy. Intelligence without shine and polish and flashiness. Ethical and principled. Frank. Wise. Well balanced. Experienced. Knowledgeable. Reasonable. Good judgement; he can see the Technocrat a mile away but he respects dreamers: "The analytic boys are a dime a dozen, but you can't buy dreams."

When in doubt, and that is almost always, choose a Craftsman. But that is the subject of Chapter Twelve. For now, it seems I may have left the impression that all is character and that therefore education has no role to play. But for me as a teacher, that would be a preposterous idea. Nothing could be further from the truth. What role, then, is left for education? Let's have a look at what nurture can do with nature.

Eleven

Notes on Education

I wish you wouldn't use words like "educational," which have grown sour from being so much in the wrong people's mouths. . . . If formal education has any bearing on the arts at all, its purpose is to make critics, not artists. Its usual effect is to cage the spirit in other people's ideas — the ideas of poets and philosophers, which were once splendid insights into the nature of life, but which people who have no insights of their own have hardened into dogmas.

REVELSTOKE IN *A MIXTURE OF FRAILTIES*,
BY ROBERTSON DAVIES

To whatever extent nurture can shape nature, we know it begins early. I would dearly like to talk about child-rearing practices, primary and secondary education, but I can't. I don't know enough about them. Like most people, I just have opinions and feelings. I think, for example, that the universal popular sentiment that something is going badly awry must have some grounding in fact. I think the instinct to restore what has been lost, captured perhaps by the expressions "discipline," "back to basics" or the "three R's," represents something profound and probably legitimate. And I am at a loss to understand why the wish to restore something of value should be seen to be regressive.

Let's say you're driving down the road and you're thinking about your work. You're a bit distracted. You miss your regular turnoff and are forced to go back. Do people scream at you, "You ought to have

171

kept going, you regressive, reactionary, antediluvian!"? Of course not. There's nothing to be ashamed of about retracing your steps if you've made a mistake. Maybe, as a society, we were distracted in the sixties and seventies and took a bunch of wrong turns. Maybe we need to retrace our steps. In any other context, this would pass for sanity, not reaction. Anyway, as I say, these are just feelings, not arguments. I have to talk about university education because, here, I have some arguments.

First, a story. Several colleagues and I recently wrote an article on decision-making and sent it off to an academic journal for publication. I don't know if you're aware of how these things work, but the editors send such a submission out to other academics for review before they accept or reject it. In due course (eighteen months), we received these evaluations and the article was accepted. But that's not the story. The story is in one of the evaluations.

In our article we had made reference to a "fifth column." One reviewer objected that we had not shown the first four columns. I had an image of this studious individual's face reddening, his eyes bugging out, his hair standing on end, veins on his temples bulging, shouting, "Fifth column! Fifth column! Where are the first four?!!" But as you and I both know, "fifth column" is an expression, a piece of symbolism we owe to the military. In fact, its specific origin is the Spanish Civil War. Franco's fascists had four columns of troops marching on democratic Madrid and were said to have a "fifth column" of spies inside the city ready to rise up and destroy democracy from within. The expression has passed into ordinary language to denote spies, subversives, ideas or people who destroy from within.

How is it that someone with the highest academic degree that can be granted — a doctorate — a supposedly highly educated person, could not know that this was symbolic, that we didn't have to list the other four? How could such a person be functionally illiterate? Because he or she has probably never read a novel, history, or philosophy, or sociology or psychology or even the newspapers. He or she has probably read nothing but management literature. *Yikes!* But if all you sociologists and psychologists think you're off the hook and I'm attacking business schools, you're dead wrong. It's a rare sociologist who knows something about psychology and a rare psychologist something about philosophy. And nobody knows anything about the Bible, either as revelation or as literature. Too many of us are "experts," trained in specialties but *uneducated*, and the problem runs very, very deep. We are the exact opposite of the ideal we all profess to admire: the Renaissance men who knew science and letters and philosophy and art. What's worse, we allow experts to dictate policy to us. For example, French historian Alain-Gérard Slama reminds us that we allow cancer researchers who have studied biochemistry and medicine to dictate public policy on smoking, and yet smoking bans raise deep philosophical issues involving subtle tradeoffs between Justice and Liberty, which cancer researchers know nothing about.[1] Well, I'm no expert on liberal-arts education, but Allan Bloom was, and anybody concerned about it should read *The Closing of the American Mind*. It sure changed the way I look at my academic world.

But I'm not here to discuss liberal-arts education either, except to say that I used to think a bachelor's degree in business was a great error. I used to think everyone should be forced to do a liberal-arts degree before we let them come to us for an advanced degree in business. This was, of course, intellectual snobbery. Ever since I found out what's going on in liberal-arts schools, I decided we can do a better job. Mark Twain, great kidder that he was, said, "Soap and education are not as sudden as a massacre, but they are more deadly in the long run." But it is water-tight specialties hardening once-splendid insights into dogmas that makes education deadly and, in our bachelor's degree in business, we escape both.

The business school, once seen by some to be the enemy of true learning, may turn out to be its salvation. The business school, at least my business school, is like what the old liberal-arts university used to be before the "great reform," before "relevance," before "expertise," before "Let the student study what she likes," before the death of "core courses." We have required courses in statistics (which our students largely hate, tsk, tsk!), and so our students don't get fooled as easily by the three lies: *lies, damn lies* and *statistics,* which parade daily in our newspapers and in our organizations. That makes better and more informed citizenship possible. Our students take mandatory business courses that are really just disguised courses in sociology, in psychology, in anthropology, in human relations. They get exposed, whether they like it or not, to philosophy, to history, to literature (not enough) and to political science, while they are learning about marketing or finance or strategy or management. And how could it be otherwise? Studying organizations and management necessitates knowing about human nature (philosophy and psychology), behaviour in different cultures (anthropology), the history of ideas (political philosophy) and of institutions (sociology). They don't get the Great Books, but who does? And besides, not everyone can benefit from the Great Books; I admit to getting a *C* in Philosophy 101. There's nothing inherently wrong with getting your great teachings through interpreters.

Yes, we also teach leadership, but not how to become a leader in five easy steps. We don't teach vision. We can't. No one can. Vision, as I hope is now clear, comes from a peculiar temperament or character (cyclothymic and autistic), and even if we wanted to, we can't train someone to be cyclothymic and autistic. You are or you aren't. Nature. But not everyone who is cyclothymic and autistic can profit from his imagination. Vision comes to the prepared mind, the mind that has been exposed to contradictions and to many different dogmas, not just one. That requires general education.

We show them vision with cases of leaders. We give them models. We try to show them how visionaries are most often manhandled by their times and by their compatriots. We try to sensitize them to the dangers of quick fixes and magic managerial formulae. We help them to discover that what you see depends on where you sit; we help them to see, I hope, that if you are a Technocrat you will see Artists as dreamers. We hope to soften this knee-jerk reaction and to bring people a little way down the long road of self-knowledge.

Thanks in part to Zaleznik, who was the first management academic to write about the nature of subordination as well as about leadership, we also teach them about craftsmanship, or "followership." In our skills courses, *Habilités de Direction*, we teach them about apprenticeship and the value and indeed the necessity of learning from others; learning to read people and situations, learning to suspend judgement, learning to despise quick fixes and recipes. The young, especially but not exclusively, need to learn to *follow* before they can *lead*. Personally, I like the old French word for apprenticeship: *compagnonnage*. *Compagnon* means, loosely, companion or fellow traveller, friend. In the context of the trades, *compagnon* is equivalent to our journeyman (notice the voyage implied). *Compagnonnage*, now replaced by *apprentissage*, once meant the whole process of learning with a companion, over an extended period, in order to become first a journeyman and then a master craftsman oneself. In the larger context, the modern word for this is mentorship, but if you don't have Craftsmen, you can't have mentors and apprentices. Mentoring requires knowledge, time, patience, forbearance, kindness and generosity of spirit. American psychoanalyst Erik Erikson calls it "generativity." It's an instinct in the old to give to the next generation; an instinct that makes ageing more bearable.

I just wonder if our schools haven't filled up, not (as it is claimed) because our students are mercenaries out to get great jobs, but because our curriculum more closely approximates the university of old. Our students are thirsty for knowledge, real knowledge. Oh, sure, some gripe and moan and balk at the requirements, but students always did and always will. But some get really turned on. Some go straight into organizations, but some leave us and go off to do degrees in philosophy, in psychology or in sociology with, I suspect, a better grounding, more real learning than students in a so-called liberal-arts program with no core courses. And that's as it should be. Since we've inherited many students from other faculties, we've inherited the corresponding obligation to educate citizens. What good to society is a marketing expert who knows nothing about ethics, or an economist who knows nothing about profound human motivations and needs?

You see, we are not offering a B.A. in administration principally to *train*, we are doing it to *educate*. We are educating young people to take their place in the world of organizations, which is the whole world, except for an infinitesimal minority who will work all alone. To accomplish this task, we need sociologists, psychologists, psychoanalysts, philosophers, statisticians, mathematicians and people with a passion for learning and for exciting young minds. And unlike academic departments in traditional universities, we all talk to each other every day. We are forced to reconcile our dogmas, or at least give place to a multiplicity of dogmas. In most schools, the literature faculty talks to the literature faculty and then apparently only about deconstructionism.[2] The economists talk only to other economists and they all seem to share a Benthamite utilitarian view of man. The sociology faculty has only fratricidal war between the socialists and the structuralists, between Marx and, let us say, Goffman. In all of these faculties, their students are forced to choose sides, adopt the authorized version. The further the student advances, the narrower and narrower he or she becomes and education turns into training.

For us, there is no authorized version. Our students are not brainwashed. Oh, some professors try — there are rascals and scoundrels everywhere — but for the most part they can't succeed. They don't have the student in their clutches long enough, and he or she is exposed to too many other versions of man. The more our students advance, from bachelors to doctorate, the broader and broader becomes their education. The world explodes.

I had been wrong. It wasn't with our undergraduate program that we had been going violently astray. It was with the MBA. Like most graduate schools of business, ours is populated by too many engineers, economists and/or undergraduate degrees in business. Now, I have absolutely nothing against engineers or economists. On the contrary, I teach them and find the vast majority to be open-minded. That's not the problem. The problem is that they're the only ones who can get past all the stiff quantitative requirements. And even if an undergraduate in humanities can get past this, he or she wouldn't want to, because we've given him the impression that management is as dull as dishwater.

No, the real problem with this is twofold. First, we don't have MBA students long enough. By the time we get them, it's largely too late to correct their already-massive biases in the short time available to us — one or two years. Second, because they come from such uniform backgrounds, they can't learn from each other. There are no historians, philosophers, psychologists in the classroom to challenge their narrow way of looking at the world. Only the professor, one lone professor, probably trapped in his own dogma (we all are, more or less). So, the MBA turns out to be largely training instead of education, and for that we are legitimately criticized.

I don't know what the answer is, but I do know we need to find one. And not because the MBA produces Technocrats. It doesn't. It can't. Nurture doesn't fundamentally change Nature. The vast majority of our MBA students are, like everywhere else, Craftsmen. But the MBA program reinforces the Technocrat, because it leaves the impression that management is about rules, maxims, numbers and paint-by-numbers art. It undermines the basic underpinning and modus operandi of craftsmanship (experience) and the source of art (imagination). It encourages the pretence that if you have an MBA and can read a balance sheet, you know how to run an organization — public or private, steel or hospital — and manage people, and that is false. Technocrats use this myth to great advantage.

My real hope, the source of my greatest optimism, is our doctoral students. Not all doctoral students in all business schools, but *Montreal* doctoral students. Montreal has a joint doctoral program in which two francophone universities — Hautes Études Commerciales (HEC) and the University of Quebec at Montreal (UQAM) — and two anglophone universities — McGill and Concordia — cooperate. That means our students are exposed to at least two ways of looking at the world, North American and European (because the French schools, HEC and UQAM, are heavily influenced by European thought). They must be bilingual, so they read material in both languages, from both traditions. And there are mandatory courses. Finance majors have to read Piaget, and psychologists have to read stuff in systems and operations research. Of course they hate to and complain all the time, but we don't listen.

Fundamental innovation comes from the confrontation of worldviews. Copernicus (you know, the sixteenth-century Polish guy who overturned the centuries-old view that the earth was the centre of the universe and that the sun and the planets orbited around the earth) was not a professional astronomer. He had a doctorate in law, and his official duties were concerned with law, administration and medicine.[3] He didn't have to support the authorized version of contemporary astronomy, because he had no students to train and did not, like professional astronomers of his day, make his living by astrological forecasts (based on the older view of the sun and planets moving around the earth). So he had no commitment to the status quo. Astronomy was, for him, a hobby, a passion, an avocation. He was what Margolis calls a "partial insider." In most domains, fundamental invention or innovation comes from people who straddle disciplines or worlds.

Our doctoral students not only straddle the francophone and anglophone worlds, their languages and cultures and ways of thinking, they also straddle the new world and the old (North America and Europe). And they straddle disciplines. We have, for example, a doctoral student who is an engineer with an MBA and is studying the career patterns of female engineers. She is a partial insider. She is reading sociology to learn how society shapes individual expectations.

She is reading both Jungian and Freudian psychology, European and North American versions. She is reading biology to understand how nature shapes nurture. I am convinced she is going to make a major contribution, not just to management, but to our world. There is no other place on earth she could get away with this. No other graduate school in the world in which she would not be obliged to adopt the authorized version of a single discipline in order to get her dissertation accepted. It will take her six to eight years of serious study (that's our average — we, too, have our dilettantes), but it will be worth every minute. Such work is exciting. It promises to revolutionize our thought. Promises to reinvigorate traditional disciplines, to break them out of their stuffy and suffocating specialties and to open up the possibility of genuine, serious, multidisciplinarity.[4] It promises artistry. It holds out the hope that the university may be restored in the public's good graces and will again be able to contribute to important public debates. The university will be able to provide, as it ought, a counterweight to what is merely popular.

And so, I have come full circle — from believing that the business school was a disaster for education to believing that it holds out enormous hope for retrieving a sense of proportion, for putting the Humpty-Dumpty of man's broken parts — utilitarian man, sociological man, psychological man, managerial man — back together again. It's time that we in business schools held our heads high in the academic world and stopped taking all this guff from the traditional disciplines. If in the past we have been part of the problem, and to some extent still are, we are also now part of the solution. Allan Bloom, can you hear me? All is not lost. We may make strange bedfellows, but we're your best hope.

Of course, we need help. The university cannot do it all. We cannot single-handedly turn back the tide if society insists on other things. We need protection. We need to be insulated from the pressure to be all things to all people, to be relevant. We must be a place of the old, of the tried and true. We cannot and should not give pride

179

of place to brand-new, shiny theories.[5] We cannot and should not respond to the businessmen who want us to train instead of to educate. That's not our job. That's what colleges are for. That's what organizations should be doing and what they in fact do when they're full of Craftsmen. Our job is to educate. We might become a city of wisdom instead of a tower of Babel:

> It is a city of wisdom, and the heart of the university is its body of learned men; it can be no better than they, and it is at their fire that the young come to warm themselves. Because the young come and go, but we remain. They are the minute-hand, we the hour-hand of the academic clock. Intelligent societies have always preserved their wise men in institutions of one kind or another, where their chief business is to be wise, to conserve the fruits of wisdom and to add to them if they can. Of course the pedants and the opportunists get in somehow, as we are constantly reminded . . . but we are the preservers and the custodians of civilization, and never more so than in the present age, where there is no aristocracy to do the job.[6]

The "preservers and custodians" cannot do that job in a society that hates preservation and custodianship, thinks only of the future and wants only what is brand-spanking-new. Wants only art. But art needs craft to bring its insights to fruition. For us to do our job, our first order of business is to help to change attitudes, to restore a respect for the Craftsman and for craftsmanship and its values. It is to that goal that I now turn. Hold on. Fasten your seat belts. I'm going to shift gears. I'm going to jump "levels of analysis," and I can hear academics all over the world shrieking, "She can't do that! She can't do that! She can't go from a study of organizations and talk about society as a whole!" No? Just watch me. Or to quote George Bush, "Read my lips."

IV

Shifting Gears to Society

Twelve An Ode to Craftsmanship

If you can keep your head when all about you
  Are losing theirs and blaming it on you,
If you can trust yourself when all men doubt you,
  But make allowance for their doubting too;
If you can wait and not be tired by waiting,
  Or being lied about, don't deal in lies,
Or being hated, don't give way to hating,
  And yet don't look too good, nor talk too wise.
If you can dream — and not make dreams your master;
  If you can think — and not make thoughts your aim;
If you can meet with Triumph and Disaster
  And treat those two impostors just the same.

RUDYARD KIPLING, *IF . . .*

Then you are a Craftsman. The absolute bedrock of civilization. Not shifted by the temporary winds and whims of change. Keeping a steady course through the tempests of time, neither lured by the sirens of passing fancy nor grounded on the reefs of the past. Knowledgeable, responsible, reasonable, sensible, trustworthy, well balanced, realistic, stable and wise, you protect us from ourselves. You are the hard principle of reality with which fantasy — artistic or technocratic — must inevitably come to terms. You've been made to feel ashamed because you are not shiny and brilliant. You don't glitter like gold or like fool's gold; you are neither Artist nor Technocrat, but you are much more than just a pale version of both. We need you now more than ever. We need you to stand up, to throw out your chest and to say, "Enough. Cut out all the chatter and let's get down to work. You, over there, sit down. You'll get your turn. You with your head in the clouds, we'll work on that tomorrow. Right now we have to get our bearings."

We have to get back to a sense of proportion and to the principles of Craftsmanship. Our world has been built by the slow accumulation of knowledge and skill, punctuated periodically by genuinely new — and, I must keep insisting, rare — insights. If you believe Darwin, nature is but a gigantic system of trial and error, of craftsmanship. Try this species. Oops. That didn't survive. Mutate. Try another.

Medicine, to take another example, is a centuries-old craft. Doctors treat patients by trial and error. A patient complains of headache. The doctor suggests Tylenol. It doesn't work. She suggests Fiorinal. It doesn't work. They do a CAT scan. It shows no abnormality. The patient is referred to a psychiatrist. It turns out the patient is a Craftsman and at work she's surrounded by Technocrats. She quits her job and the headaches disappear. What doctor worth her salt would have *started* with exploratory neurosurgery? Open up someone's head just in case? Quick fixes. Medical science as a whole learns slowly, by trial and error, and occasionally leaps forward with a new insight. It's a painstaking process. We try not to hurry new drugs onto the market, for example, because they may do more harm than good. Remember Thalidomide.

In fact, all science is built largely on trial and error. A genius like Copernicus comes along with a new insight and the next years and even centuries are spent doing what Thomas Kuhn called "normal science." Craftsmanship. Working out the bugs and the specific implications of the new insight. Until another genius comes along and breaks the gestalt and everyone has to unlearn what they thought they already knew.

Teaching is a craft; I know, because I'm still learning it every day from my colleagues. I have graduated from apprentice to journeyman,

184

but they are the master craftsmen. You cannot *tell* someone how to be a teacher. He or she has to do it under (yes, I said *under*) the patient, tolerant guidance of a master. I have to watch them, listen to them, trust them, follow them. Oh, to be sure, there are a few "born teachers," Artists who just have an instinct for it. But they're rare. You can be the most brilliant academic in the world and an utter flop at teaching. If someone, say, a Technocrat, comes along to try to tell me that he has a new way to revolutionize teaching, I will listen with a very sceptical ear. And if some futurist tells me that the classroom is about to be replaced by palm-top computers, I shall weep bitter tears of dread. And I will resist. Violently. Human beings are actors and creators. We don't have to follow the trends. We can change them. We can put the lie to them all.

Entrepreneurship, too, is largely a craft. Owner-managers of small and medium-size businesses are, for the most part, Craftsmen. They have translated experience, a skill, a *métier*, into a business, usually by identifying some relatively small but important innovation in product or service. The ones who innovate on a grand scale, the really big success stories, are invariably Artists. And among the millions and millions of startups, these big stories are rare indeed. Some of them get killed off prematurely when a Technocrat is given too much power to put some order into the shop.

Managing organizations and managing people is a craft. Not an art and most certainly not a science. Rejuvenating organizations may be an Art. Managing things, or thinglike aspects of organizations, may be a science. But the craft of managing people takes wisdom, patience, experience, authority, conviction, realism. And what does the future hold? The best predictor of tomorrow's weather is today's weather. If it's sunny today, the odds are better than fifty-fifty that it'll be sunny tomorrow. Tomorrow, most of us are still going to go into the office, into the school, into the lab, into the factory. While the future designs itself, we still have to work and to live. What we've been doing for the past few years is probably what we'll be doing for the next few years.

And that's good, not bad. We need stability for healthy change. I know that sounds paradoxical and maybe it is. But let me give an example of what I mean. Heroin addicts commit crime to support their habit. When they are in the throes of the addiction, when they need a fix, they can't think straight. Heroin substitution programs, like methadone, are designed to give the addict some stability, some calm, so that he or she can make a rational decision to change. When you're strung out, living in chaos and crisis, you do not behave rationally. In our organizations, we need the honest, trustworthy, calm authority of the experienced Craftsman to be able to behave rationally, to be able to recognize and promote artistry when it comes along, to be able to recognize Technocrats and to have the legitimate authority to keep them in their place, to keep their technical virtuosity and brilliance subservient to larger social goals. Former French prime minister Georges Clemenceau said that war was a much too serious thing to be left to the military. Well, managing is a much too serious thing to be left to self-styled professional managers.

So the Craftsman looks at the new tools, for that is what they are, coming out of the management literature and says, not no, but maybe. Reengineering? Flat structures? Maybe, I'll have my best Technocrat take a look at it. Alliances? Maybe, I'll give it some thought. The information revolution, you say. Maybe, but "where is the wisdom we have lost in knowledge, where is the knowledge we have lost in information?"[1]

Remember our Craftsmen Jeb, Robert and Rodney? They said things like, "People are the organization's biggest asset," "You have to invest in the people and the profit follows," "You can't change everything overnight. It takes time to weld a group of people together." They say most of the things we want to hear. But they said maybe to the Technocrats' brilliant schemes and got fired for it. And the organization went belly-up because it changed its structures and its personnel too much — not too little. Not because it went too slowly, but because it went too fast. It lurched from one piece of shiny new rhetoric to the next.

The Craftsman is the preserver and the mentor. Since when have realism and conviction become outmoded, old-fashioned? He's the one who will give our young people, most of whom are budding Craftsmen, a chance to get started. He's the one who will accept them into the organization even if they are not "brilliant." He won't ask them if they are charismatic. He doesn't expect them to be. He will ask them what they *know* and whether they have the desire to *learn how to do*. He's the one who will mentor, empower and teach and train and invest in them. The Artist hasn't got the time. And the Technocrat hasn't got the inclination.

When you are driving in the fog, do you speed up? When you are lost, do you run? We have got to slow down, not speed up. We may have to go backward as well as forward. Here's T. S. Eliot:

> We shall not cease from exploration
> And the end of all our exploring
> Will be to arrive where we started
> And know the place for the first time

Why race headlong, like a car careering out of control, into a future that no one, no one, can know? It feels to me that that's what we're doing with our organizations and with society as a whole. Careering out of control. Rudderless. Pretending to know everything about the future and knowing nothing about the past. Everybody's reading the futurists and nobody's reading Plato, and yet, he could have told us. The same Santayana who told us that "man's progress has a poetic phase in which he imagines the world" told us, if we had only listened to him in 1905, "Progress, far from consisting in change, depends on retentiveness. . . . Those who cannot remember the past are condemned to repeat it."

I'm shifting gears again. Right into overdrive. Let's talk about the larger implications of all this for some social and economic issues.

Thirteen　Some Social and Economic Implications

> Things fall apart; the centre cannot hold;
> Mere anarchy is loosed upon the world,
> The blood-dimmed tide is loosed, and everywhere
> The ceremony of innocence is drowned;
> The best lack all conviction, while the worst
> Are full of passionate intensity.
>
> W. B. Yeats, *The Second Coming*

But, you say, we can't wait for craftsmanship. It's too slow. We have a school system that's gone to the dogs. We have an environment that's decaying around us. We have a health system we can't afford. There's no work. We're choking in government deficits and children are drowning in poverty. There's no day care and women have to work. Divorce is on the rise and the wolf is at the door.

Calm down.

When you're in a bad mood or a sad mood, all you can remember are bad things and sad things. G. H. Bower, an award-winning American experimental psychologist, has been working on the relations between emotion, or affect, and thought, mood and memory. Here's an example of what he discovers:

> We found powerful effects of people's moods on the free associations they gave to neutral words. For instance, a subject who was happy was given the stimulus word *life* and gave as chained free associates the

words *love, freedom, fun, open,* and *joy.* Another subject who was angry responded with the associates *struggle, toil, fight,* and *compete.*

Well, some of us are angry and some of us are depressed, but collectively we have all lost our heads. Some individuals and families are in crisis, but collectively in the West we are *not.* We are not at war and we do not need desperate measures. Yugoslavia is in crisis; people are dying. Parts of Africa are in crisis; people are dying. The Middle East is in a state of crisis as I write; people are dying. The Jews went through a crisis during World War II; millions died. Please let's not minimize what all the above went through or are going through by imagining that what we are going through is in any way comparable. Let us not take all the meaning out of the word "crisis." The more people repeat that we are in crisis, the more we risk actually being in one. But even if I am wrong and we are in a genuine crisis, what do we do? In the subway, we're told, "In case of accident, stay calm. Follow instructions." In a fire, they tell us, "Stay calm. Follow instructions." In an airplane, "Stay calm. Follow the pilot's instructions."

I don't wish to minimize the profound challenges with which we are faced or to minimize the sense of emergency some feel. Emergency, we know, is a subjective thing. Doctors have always had to struggle with defining what constitutes an emergency. When a frightened patient comes into an emergency room, they check him over and, if they find nothing wrong, they do *not* dismiss him or his fears. A good doctor will try to reassure him: "Yes. I understand. You had a right to be frightened. It could have been very serious. Fortunately it wasn't. But what you need to do now is go home and get some rest. You've had a bad scare."

All right. We've had a bad scare. We thought the GNP would grow continuously the way it used to. We thought our young people would find easy entry into the job market the way most of us did. (But, I remind you, the way our grandfathers did not.) In the sixties we had what sociologists used to call "a revolution of rising expectations" and now, in the nineties, we're having a "revolution of declining expectations," and it hurts. But it's not the end of the world; it just sometimes feels like it. If we lose our heads, we won't find the solutions we need to find. If we go off half-cocked and buy harebrained schemes and quick fixes, we'll do no one any good and a lot of people a lot of harm. We have got to stop asking for miracles and oracles. We have got to get our feet back on the ground.

When we ask our all-too-human politicians for instant solutions, what do we risk getting? Technocratic answers or madness. Governing, too, is a craft — not an art and not a science. Every once in a while we get Artists, or statesmen, but mostly we get Craftsmen. Most of them are honest, intelligent and sincere. They work in teams and most have democratic instincts. If we give them time and our thoughtful responses, they will arrive at decent, humane approaches. If we press them to solve all our problems all at once, they will have no choice but to come up with ill-thought-out programs and policies or technocratic solutions that will please no one. The Weimar Republic was in a hurry and it got Hitler. Authoritarianism breeds insecurity; we look for a saviour and we get a madman. We have to calm down, if only to prevent that.

Then what should we do about the big issues? What about the economy, for example? I don't know and, if you do, think again. We have lost too many signposts, too many *isms*: the Phillips curve, Keynesian*ism*, Friedman*ism*. We are in a new context with the collapse of the Berlin Wall, the rise of Japan, the speed of information and globalization, and the death throes and aftermath of the disintegration of the U.S.S.R. This last, the disintegration of the Soviet Union, is, I think, the biggest one. And, it's the biggest one, not only because of the social and economic implications, but also because of the philosophic ones. With the collapse of the crucible of the communist experiment, social democrats have been discredited along with the communists. Anything that smacks of the role of government has a bad smell to it.

And yet, what do we have to take its place but cowboy capitalism? I don't think there are more than a handful of Canadians, Swiss, Swedes or Germans who would trade their social stability, their health-care systems, for the dubious benefits of an American-style capitalism that leaves too many sick, homeless and violent. Here is a more typical European view:

> In America we see scenes reminiscent of certain underdeveloped countries of the southern hemisphere; . . . lines of unemployed on the sidewalk, two steps away from insolent, luxurious boutiques; the homeless hanging around doorsteps surrounded by overturned garbage; middle-class America impoverished more and more; private police and bodyguards, one of the rare growth sectors, while ordinary Americans arm themselves to the teeth . . . and the rate of homicide of young men in major cities ranges from 4 to 73 times higher than Bangladesh, one of the poorest countries in the world.[1]

On the other hand, the resilience of the American economy, its entrepreneurship and level of innovation, its deep and efficient capital markets, are the envy of the world, and rightly so.

All around the western world, there is a largely futile battle going on, with the advocates of government and social programs on one side, and the deficit fighters on the other, as though these were the only two options: sacrifice everything to get the deficit and the debt under control, or save everything and to hell with the deficit. But this is madness. Utter madness. And it didn't have to happen. This debt thing didn't sneak up on anybody. It was growing evident by the mid-seventies. Many tried to tell our governments, but they wouldn't listen. They were trapped in Keynesian ideology and their opponents were trapped in Friedmanite ideology, and so lacked all credibility. A craft attitude would be: Keynes is right; Friedman is right; America is right; Germany is right; Japan is right. Let's take the best from them all. Let's adapt others' insights to our aspirations and capacities.

Michel Albert, an intelligent and wise French businessman, has written a delightful book called *Capitalisme contre Capitalisme* (capitalism versus capitalism), in which he pleads with his countrymen not to follow Britain's headlong rush to imitate America. A businessman who publicly defends the role of the state — what next? France, he feels, is being seduced by American-style capitalism, forgetting both its own traditions and the example of its most powerful neighbour, Germany. Until communism collapsed, many looked to Germany as the economic, social-democratic miracle. The size of the state in relation to the gross national product was much higher than our own. And yet the German mark climbed and climbed in noninflationary value. Hard-money policy did that, a sober lesson learned from the disastrous Weimar experience, and a lesson we, too, have thankfully and finally learned.

There are two parts to the size of government equation — a numerator and a denominator, if you will. The numerator is the weight of government; the denominator is the strength of the private sector that supports it. The German private sector was capable of supporting a lot of weight. Even in these difficult times, Germany has chosen to undertake the most massive social-redemption project on earth: the $100 billion reunification of the country. How?

Well, let's think a minute about Germany. In fact, let's use an example, since mental pictures are worth at least five hundred, if not a thousand, words. Think about a Mercedes-Benz car. What's the first thing that comes to mind? Expensive? That's for sure, but why? A status symbol, you say? Certainly, but why? Because it costs a lot of money. Yes, but why does it cost a lot of money? Quality = durability = resale value = customer loyalty = word-of-mouth sales = lower advertising budgets = higher engineering budgets = higher quality = durability = a virtuous circle. Listen to this 1965 Mercedes ad campaign:

> Mercedes is a maverick among car-builders. While most auto manu-
> facturers design cars to satisfy their "marketing men," we build cars

to satisfy our engineers. The sales experts in Detroit say we're out of our minds, but we're absolutely convinced that our engineers know more about building great cars than the men who study merchandising and promotion.[2]

That's 1965, not 1995! Nobody told them about total quality management. They just did it. It was second nature, but at the time, Detroit was riding high and what Mercedes said and did was blasphemous. Since then, of course, Mercedes has had to learn some marketing lessons, and Detroit, some quality lessons.

Is a Mercedes sexy? Flashy? Can you tell the difference between the 1988 model and today's? I can't. Stylistic changes have been minimal. That's one of the reasons, along with durability, resale value holds up; next year's model doesn't make last year's model look old-fashioned. But there have been tons of innovation, mostly invisible to the untrained eye. The door handle, for example, looks old-fashioned — just an ordinary-looking handle that all cars used to have. But guess what? If you're in an accident, that door handle can be pried open more easily than the newer, fancier designs. That might save your life. Inside the handle, invisible, is a small counterweight mechanism that ensures against the door popping open during an accident. That, too, might save your life. All right. I'll stop there because I'm not trying to sell Mercedes-Benz cars. I'm trying to provide a metaphor for the merits of craftsmanship — quality, excellence, experience, experimentation, innovation on a human scale. I suspect the company has had visionaries in its present or in its past, but I don't know. I do know, however, that this cult of excellence would not have been possible if the company had been run by Technocrats, because in 1965 the Technocrats would have imitated Detroit — conventional wisdom of the day — and killed it. (Incidentally, Mercedes never seemed to have much trouble penetrating the so-called closed Japanese market.)

The cult of excellence is sustained by a craft culture, which values tradition and apprenticeship. In Germany (or in Japan, for that matter) it is a rare executive who even gets into middle management before his forties, and rarer still is an executive who has not come up through the ranks of his industry. Until very recently, before the impact of the recession and the reintegration of East Germany, youth unemployment was minimal. The great majority of young people went into apprenticeship programs and got trained to do useful tasks and learned the value of "precision, punctuality and reliability."[3] All right, I'm not here to sing the praises of the German model, either, except to say that it *is* one; I don't want to live there, either. I want to live here. But I want us to learn from everyone.

Strengthening the private sector is just as important as reducing the public sector, but reduce it we must. Not because of some ridiculous ideology, but because the private sector is too weak to carry the load. Taxes are too high and we have to rethink everything. Programs are contradictory, redundant, out of date, and not because we've lacked Artists or Technocrats, but because we've lacked Craftsmen. One of the leitmotifs of craftsmanship is gradual adaptation. Things don't get out of date, because their utility is constantly reassessed. If the tool gets dull, sharpen it. The craft attitude is to cut off the branch to save the tree. Regular pruning. Of course, to prune a tree, you have to know what you're doing. If you cut too many branches, the tree won't grow strong and straight; it will die.

So for now we have to prune the public sector because the debt is killing us, crippling our capacity to act. Reality not ideology. (If we could afford to pay ourselves the best systems in the world, it would de desirable, not undesirable.) We need a spirit of experimentation in all domains, a spirit of craftsmanship that says: "This worked in the past, and this didn't; let's try something new." Of course, we need imagination, and let's hope some Artist will come up with some big new synthesis we can all get to work on. But while we're waiting, let's do some small, sane things and stop shouting at one another.

Before I conclude, I want to have a private word with my generation. I won't be long.

Fourteen ∎ Baby Boomers: On "Cocooning"

Come Mothers and Fathers throughout the land,
And don't criticize what you can't understand,
Your sons and your daughters are beyond your command
Your old world is rapidly fading
Please, get out of the new one if you can't lend a hand,
For the times they are a-changin'.

                BOB DYLAN, *THE TIMES THEY ARE A-CHANGIN'*

Do you recognize this song? Bob Dylan was the hero of the sixties. We loved him. We worshipped him. This song, I think, more than any other, captures the spirit of that age of idealism and destructiveness. Why destructiveness? you ask. Because, while they were already decaying, we are the ones who undermined, fatally, the legitimate authority structures that are vital to a preservation of craftsmanship. We laughed and applauded while a University of Toronto student punched a dean in the face during a commencement ceremony. We called policemen pigs. We manned the barricades to destroy scholarship by making education "relevant." We told our mothers and fathers to get out of the way, and God only knows why, they did! *They have sown the wind, and they shall reap the whirlwind.*[1] How do you like what we have sown? Do you like the relevant education system that we demanded and got? Do you like not being able to influence your adolescent children? We taught them the language of rights, but we left out responsibility. Recently adolescents in France took to the streets

195

to intimidate a government, to demand their "rights" to satisfying jobs. No one told them that a satisfying job is not a right but a privilege and one that few enjoy. No one told them that government can't give what it hasn't got. These adolescents, screeching for their rights, have been compared with the adolescents of 1968 who were screaming for the rights of others: Chilean and Vietnamese peasants, Mississippi blacks, California farm workers. I resent the comparison.

After Paris circa 1968, after Kent State, after Chile's Allende was murdered by the forces of darkness, we lost heart, and now, it is said, we're "cocooning." Let's take that metaphor to its logical conclusion. In the cycle of metamorphosis, it all starts with eggs. Ours were laid in the postwar period of rising prosperity. The next stage is a larva, a wormlike creature, that burrows and bores its way into, say, a leaf. When it is finished, the leaf is destroyed, killed. Wanting with good reason to rid the world of authoritarianism, we bored our way into all of society's legitimate authority structures — the family, the church, the government, the police, the school — and destroyed them. I remember someone asking me when I was thirteen if I wanted to study Latin. I puffed myself up with a big adult voice and cried, "Latin. Latin is a dead language! I want to study something relevant." Well, I was a child; the real mistake was not mine but that of the people who let me make it. Anyway, now it is said that we are in the stage of the pupa, the cocoon. Having "sown the wind," having "loosed anarchy in the land," we have the nerve to hole up somewhere and not try to right what we have destroyed? *The best have lost all conviction, while the worst are full of passionate intensity.*

No. The story is not finished. A cocoon is a safe shelter, a safe hiding place in which the larva, the caterpillar, takes nourishment and grows. Soon he will emerge a butterfly, an adult. An adult takes responsibility. And all of we baby boomers have a responsibility to leave the cocoon and assume the adult burden of what we have done. Yes, I know. It's scary to go out in the whirlwind we have sown, easier to lie back and watch *Roseanne*. Easier, but irresponsible.

Back in the sixties, the worst insult we could hurl at anyone was "Personalist!" Remember? We accused anybody who was not part of the fight, anybody who studied or got married and raised a family, of being a traitor, a personalist who put his own petty little personal life before the great social struggle. Have you all become personalists? Speak up.

Stand up and be counted. Say something.

In Conclusion . . .

It was the best of times, it was the worst of times, it was the age of wisdom, it was the age of foolishness, it was the epoch of belief, it was the epoch of incredulity, it was the season of Light, it was the season of Darkness, it was the spring of hope, it was the winter of despair, we had everything before us, we had nothing before us, we were all going direct to Heaven, we were all going direct the other way. . . .
CHARLES DICKENS, *A TALE OF TWO CITIES*

Those words were written in 1859. Well, *Plus ça change, plus c'est la même chose* — the more things change, the more they stay the same. It still is, as it is in every age, the best of times and the worst of times. Such is the human dilemma. To live with doubt and ambiguity and uncertainty and to forge ahead anyway. As Malcolm Muggeridge said of his religion, faith is not the absence of doubt but its acceptance.

Sure times are tough and confusing. Big, once invincible corporate giants and governments are having to live in a world that smaller businesses and institutions, and the vast majority of citizens, have always inhabited. A world without guarantees and a world that demands a sharp pencil, vigilance and constant innovation. Their technocratic illusions have caught up with them; things don't stay the same for very long. So, the wrenching downsizing, restructuring, is going on. Some of these giants will need Artists at the top to find a new vision. Some will need Craftsmen to put an end to their delusions of grandeur and to get back to basics. Those whose backs are truly to the wall may even need, temporarily, a hardnosed, brilliant Technocrat at the helm to chop and hack their way to survival.

And while all this is going on, people are being laid off — but not at Microsoft. The new economy is designing itself, and like always, the new jobs are coming from the new players. Some of them will be Artists; some Craftsmen. None will be Technocrats (or if they are, they won't survive). In that respect, North America, with its high rate of new venture formation, is the favourite for those with betting instincts. I don't think we should throw in the towel.

When I decided to take this trip, this search, this *re*search, it was because I was angry and frustrated. I saw the Technocrats. I saw what they were doing and I wanted to prove that their recipes, their smug self-satisfaction, their pious phrases and their sermonettes were dangerous. I wanted to show what I had often seen, that artistry existed in management. That dreams sometimes come true. Like most people, I, too, saw the world in black and white; leaders versus managers, if you will. I didn't know, I couldn't know, that I would find the Craftsman and discover that he had been made invisible by this polarization of our thinking. But isn't that what research is supposed to be about? Finding things. Looking into the past to shed light on the present.

But not to forecast it into the future. I don't know if, as the new millennium opens, we are at the dawning of a new age. If we are, I don't know if it will be a renaissance of craftsmanship and of Craftsmen — of skill, *métier*, realism, wisdom, conviction and legitimate authority. But I hope so, because Craftsmen will give Artists room to breathe and time to create, and they will keep Technocrats in their legitimate place. I do know that we have a say in the matter. The future is not in a trend-line; the future is us. So, I say, *Craftsmen of the world unite; you have nothing to lose but your chains!*

Technical Appendix

The adjective checklist (ACL) was administered in the interview context. Observers — peers, subordinates and board members — were asked to check as many adjectives as they thought applied to the fifteen target subjects — all CEOs. They were instructed to respond quickly and spontaneously to the stimulus words, keeping in mind dominant traits of the person in question. For example, although most people may be characterized as punctual, it is not necessarily something that automatically springs to mind with certain individuals. The objective was to delineate core characteristics. All subjects cooperated fully. Administration was adjusted continuously throughout this phase of the research to ensure balance in representation and to guard against systematic bias. That is, as results were analysed successively, each target executive was judged by an equal mix of Artists, Craftsmen, and Technocrats. Complete administration resulted in a database of nine thousand responses.

ANALYSIS

When all the results were tallied, I was confronted with a matrix of nine thousand data points. Visual inspection of the data seemed to confirm, in general, the hypothesis of three distinct groups. However, especially with a database of this size, perceptual bias is a serious obstacle; recency, saliency, prior schema processing all potentially interfere with or distort the emerging portrait (Hogarth and Makridakis, 1981; Tversky and Kahneman, 1981). Anomalies can be overlooked, important secondary trends, obscured. The data were, therefore, subjected to more formal analytic techniques, namely, factor analysis and correspondence analysis.

Factor Analysis

Factor analysis is a technique in widespread use; Kerlinger calls it "the queen of analytic methods" (1986:569). Used as a data-reduction technique to search for mysterious underlying uniformities or clusters, or as an hypothesis-testing device to confirm or infirm a priori notions, it has proved to be an invaluable tool. In the present case, it offers a way to circumvent the perceptual bias noted above. The conceptual and mathematical underpinnings of factor analysis are well explained elsewhere (Kerlinger, 1986; Overall and Klett, 1972), but in lay terms the technique consists of using correlation analysis to compute constructs or "factors" underlying several variables or tests.

In standard R-type factor analysis, we would reduce our sixty adjectives into several groups that are highly correlated internally but weakly correlated with each other. Our interest, however, lies more with finding resemblances, not between adjectives, but between people. That is, we wished to test the hypothesis that there was a determinate number of groups of individuals who could, within the constraints of the definitions cited earlier, be described as Artists, Craftsmen and Technocrats. This necessitated performing Q-type factor analysis (Overall and Klett, 1972; Miller and Friesen, 1980), reversing rows and columns in the matrix, replacing variables with people. Overall and Klett (1972:203) speak to a controversial point with respect to Q-type analyses:

> . . . the partitioning of individuals does not appear at first blush to make much sense. Within the context of the linear factor model, however, it is quite reasonable to conceive of "person factors" as *ideal types* and the factor loadings as indices of relationship of individuals to the several ideal types.

The factor analysis was accomplished using the statistical package for the social sciences (SPSS) "factor" program with principal components extraction and rotation to simple solution. A "simple" solution is one in which each variable, in our case each person, is loaded mainly on one factor, and there are many negligible loadings in the factor matrix (Kerlinger, 1986:581). We present here, in summary form, the last steps. Initially we find the global results and their levels of "significance," followed by the final "oblique" solution.

The first thing to note is that, with a generally accepted cutoff limit of 1 (one) for acceptable eigenvalues, the procedure resulted in three factors that together accounted for 75.1% of the overall variance. Table 1 presents the results.

TABLE 1: INITIAL STATISTICS

VARIABLE	COMMUNALITY	FACTOR	EIGENVALUE	% OF VAR	CUM%
James	1	1	5.24322	35.0	35.0
Cobb	1	2	3.56595	23.8	58.7
Mike	1	3	2.46318	16.4	75.1
Ross	1	4	.91179	6.1	81.2
Peter	1	5	.58398	3.9	85.1
Cam	1	6	.55231	3.7	88.8
Judd	1	7	.35192	2.3	91.1
Brien	1	8	.31449	2.1	93.2
David	1	9	.25667	1.7	95.0
Rodney	1	10	.15990	1.1	96.0
Robert	1	11	.14663	1.0	97.0
George	1	12	.13759	.9	97.9
Rowan	1	13	.12562	.8	98.8
Bill	1	14	.10685	.7	99.5
Jeb	1	15	.07989	.5	100.0

It is clear that we had three strong factors with solid eigenvalues. It remained to rotate the data to simple solution. An "oblique" rotation presumes that the factors are somewhat correlated. As between orthogonal and oblique rotations, there is no generally accepted "correct" procedure, it being largely "a matter of taste" (Kerlinger,1986:582).

203

THE FINAL SOLUTION

As predicted, the pure Craftsmen, Robert, Jeb, George and Rodney, loaded highly — respectively, .94, .92, .90 and .86 — and solely on factor one, which we dubbed the Craftsman Ideal Type.

Cobb, Mike and James loaded, respectively, .88, .87 and .78, on factor two, which we called the Artist Ideal Type. James shows a lesser but still interesting loading on the craft factor, at .31, which confirms that the Artist may contain significant Craftsman-like qualities.

As expected, David, Ross and Peter loaded highly on factor three, the Technocrat Ideal Type, measuring, respectively, .83, .68 and .67. Ross shows interesting loadings on the art factor, at .32, indicating that a Technocrat may have artistic leanings or elements, and loaded negatively on the craft factor at -.34. He is the only Technocrat to load negatively on craft, but he is not the only one to display anti-craft characteristics. The two other Technocrats loading, respectively, .65 and .59 on the third factor are Cam and Judd. Their results are fascinating, since they load almost as strongly on the art factor but in a negative direction. Their results show most strongly the polarity between the two ideal types.

Bill and Rowan were somewhat enigmatic during observation and interviews such that it was unclear whether they were predominantly Artists or Craftsmen. The results here confirm the earlier confusion, with Bill loading quite highly on craft at .84 but loading significantly, at .36, on factor two, art. Rowan, on the other hand, loads only on craft, but more weakly at .52. This result was unsurprising in a sense, because it became clear during the interviews that there were radically different opinions of him. The results therefore tended to cancel out.

Finally, the anomalous, in the sense of unpredicted, result for Brien. He was predicted to fall firmly in the Technocrat Ideal Type but, in fact, loads more highly on the craft factor at .68, compared to .40. Like Technocrats Cam and Judd, however, he loads highly negatively on art at -.55. Table 2 presents the results.

Variable	Craftsman	Artist	Technocrat
Robert	.93262		
Jeb	.91573		
George	.89821		
Rodney	.86353		
Bill	.83884	.32296	
Brien	.68253	-.54930	.40238
Rowan	.52813		
Cobb		.88454	
Mike		.87064	
James	.31343	.77761	
David			.83254
Ross	-.33603	.32420	.68479
Peter			.67010
Cam		-.62962	.64522
Judd	.40150	-.58312	.58617

Note: Loadings under .3 have been suppressed for improved legibility.

Discussion

Globally, these results were highly satisfying. Three strong factors, and not six or seven or two, emerged as hypothesized. The individuals who loaded on the factors were, with one exception, predicted. Anomalies are, of course, unsurprising. After all, we are dealing with people and not with objects. The factors represent ideal types to which real individuals will be expected to conform only "more or less." To understand the anomalies one is forced back to the raw data. When we compare, for example, the portrait of a pure Craftsman with that of Brien, we discover that they are correlated at .6950 ($p. < .01$). But, and this is more important, along what dimensions are they correlated or, more precisely, in what ways are they both alike and dissimilar? It turns out that both Brien and Judd share with the Craftsman his conventionalism, his emotional stability, but depart radically from him with respect to the qualities of warmth, humaneness, generosity. This leads to a more general point about the factor analysis. As helpful as it is and as gratifying the results seem to be, it nonetheless left too many questions unanswered. Because we cannot, simultaneously, view the people, the ideal types and the adjectives that served to create those types, we are forced into a still-intuitive and visual inspection of a large database. For this reason, we turned to a less well-known (in North America) European analytic technique called "correspondence analysis." Its graphic outputs allowed us to better explain both the factors and the anomalies.

CORRESPONDENCE ANALYSIS

The conceptual and mathematical bases of correspondence analysis are explained, in detail, elsewhere (Fenelon, 1981; Lebart, Morineau and Warwick, 1984). In short, it uses a distance measure to allow the "simultaneous representation of two data sets" and is best applied to data consisting of contingency tables and binary coding (Lebart, Morineau and Warwick, 1984:30). Our data are precisely of this contingent nature: for example, "If you are Brien, how likely are you to be seen as visionary?" The output of correspondence analysis is also factors, but factors that have been created simultaneously by the weight of both the adjectives and the individuals. We are able to see the mathematical contribution of each individual and each adjective to the factor, and the final graphic display places all the data before our eyes. We will proceed as we did with factor analysis, reporting first the overall statistics and moving to successively greater detail.

INITIAL STATISTICS

Like principal-components analysis, correspondence analysis produces factors and associated eigenvalues. It does not, however, cut off the creation of factors according to the strength of those eigenvalues. In these initial statistics we see, therefore, all conceivable factors even though they contribute little explanatory power with respect to the overall variance in the data. The principal thing to note is that, as in the factor analysis, the first three factors account for the same amount of variance, around seventy-five percent. The first two factors are overwhelmingly dominant, accounting for forty-two and twenty-seven percent for a total of sixty-nine.

TABLE 3: CORRESPONDENCE ANALYSIS INITIAL STATISTICS

FACTOR	EIGENVALUE	% OF VARIANCE	CUM % OF VARIANCE
1	0.18360	41.759	41.759
2	0.12068	27.449	69.208
3	0.02854	6.490	75.699
4	0.02305	5.244	80.942
5	0.01448	3.293	84.235
6	0.01410	3.207	87.442
7	0.01189	2.704	90.147
8	0.01057	2.405	92.551
9	0.00752	1.711	94.262
10	0.00681	1.550	95.812
11	0.00567	1.289	97.101
12	0.00523	1.189	98.290
13	0.00415	0.945	99.235
14	0.00337	0.765	100.00

As with principal-components analysis, correspondence analysis requires knowledgeable interpretive effort to bear fruit. Unlike its North American counterpart, it does not use rotations to arrive at the "best" solution. The interpretive effort lies, instead, in inspection of the composition of the factors, the contributions of both rows (the adjectives) and columns (the people), to their creation, and inspection of the graphic representations of the factors, two-by-two, in two-dimensional space. The whole of that interpretive process will not be presented here. Here we present the final results.

WHAT AND WHO CREATED FACTOR ONE?

It is important to remember that with this analytic technique both positive and negative contributions count. That is, certain adjectives are mathematically attracted to each other and repelled by others. Similarly, certain people are similar, are attracted to each other, and others are repelled, mathematically. A factor in this case is a linear vector in space whose position is influenced by all other factors, individuals and adjectives. We have seen from the initial statistics that factor one is highly significant, accounting for more than forty percent of overall variance in the data. Factor one is, let us say, composed of adjectives and people. In terms of mathematical weight or mass, it was created by, in order of importance, Cobb, Mike, James, and Ross and influenced negatively by, in order, Brien, Rodney, Judd, Robert and Cam. It is clearly our art vector or ideal type. With the positive contribution of our Artists from the factor analysis and the negative contribution of our Technocrat Ideal Type, it shows even more clearly the polarity between the two styles. Interestingly, it also shows the negative contribution of two Craftsmen. The reason for this will become clearer below, but for now let us say that the Craftsman repels the Artist because, in some important respects, they are very different. Table 4 presents the summary results.

TABLE 4: THE PEOPLE AND FACTOR ONE

POSITIVE		NEGATIVE	
PERSON	CONTRIBUTION	PERSON	CONTRIBUTION
Cobb	232	Brien	-106
Mike	157	Rodney	-88
James	101	Judd	-71
Ross	79	Robert	-69

Note: The software ADDAD uses a base of 1000.

As was true for people, so it is true for the adjectives. Some adjectives associate positively with the art vector, and others, negatively. With positive associations we find, in order, bold, daring, intuitive, exciting, volatile, unpredictable and entrepreneurial. Conversely, conventional, meticulous, controlled and methodical are strongly repelled. This begins to explain why the Craftsmen, Rodney and Robert, should have contributed negatively to the factor. A Craftsman is seldom described as bold and unpredictable. The Technocrat, on the other hand, is often described as conventional and, above all, meticulous. It is the richness of the simultaneous treatment in correspondence analysis that allows us to capture these nuances. The results are presented in Table 5.

TABLE 5: THE ADJECTIVES AND FACTOR ONE

POSITIVE		NEGATIVE	
ADJECTIVE	CONTRIBUTION	ADJECTIVE	CONTRIBUTION
bold	71	conventional	-39
daring	55	controlled	-34
intuitive	54	meticulous	-31
exciting	51	methodical	-30
volatile	46		
unpredictable	43		
entrepreneurial	41		

These results are, in themselves, fascinating, but they become more illuminating with each successive juxtaposition of other results. Factor two, as we have seen, contributes importantly to the explanation of overall variance. Its shape must, therefore, have much to tell us. We proceed to an interpretation of those results followed immediately by the juxtaposition of the two factors in space. Factor three will not be elucidated since it does not contribute materially to our understanding.

WHAT AND WHO CREATED FACTOR TWO?

Factor two contributes twenty-seven percent to the explanation of overall variance. It is shaped, largely, by ten individuals and ten adjectives. In terms of positive contribution, and once again in order of importance, it is formed by Cam, Ross, David, Judd and Peter — our Technocrats from the SPSS analysis. The vector was influenced negatively by Bill, Jeb, Robert, James, and George: three pure Craftsmen, one Craftsman with an artistic strain and one artist with craftlike humanism. Here we see the polarity between the Technocrat and the Craftsman along, let us say, a temperament dimension. Table 6 gives the highlights.

TABLE 6: THE PEOPLE AND FACTOR TWO

POSITIVE		NEGATIVE	
PERSON	CONTRIBUTION	PERSON	CONTRIBUTION
Cam	211	Bill	-98
Ross	140	Jeb	-84
David	100	Robert	-62
Judd	70	James	-54
Peter	63	George	-36

The individuals who influence the vector tell one kind of story, but the adjectives embellish and enliven that story. In the case of factor two, the five strongly, positively associated adjectives are: difficult, hardheaded, distant, stiff and uncompromising; those most strongly negatively associated are: humane, amiable, warm, helpful and generous. The vector appears to produce a sort of thermometer, a continuum, which ranges from warm to cold, from the most pure Craftsman to the most pure Technocrat. Table 7 shows the relative contributions.

TABLE 7: THE ADJECTIVES AND FACTOR TWO

POSITIVE		NEGATIVE	
ADJECTIVE	CONTRIBUTION	ADJECTIVE	CONTRIBUTION
difficult	64	humane	-41
hardheaded	57	amiable	-36
distant	50	warm	-31
stiff	46	helpful	-30
uncompromising	38	generous	-30

It is worth emphasizing that these analytical procedures are producing constructs, ideal types, and that real people would seldom find themselves positioned neatly along one or another continuum. Constructs do, however, help to impose useful order on an otherwise incomprehensible world. Several constructs or ideal types taken together can help us to position and understand more clearly the real individuals who have made up this organization. Placing factors one and two together in two dimensions adds necessary and revealing complexity to the portrait we are drawing, and correspondence analysis, treating as it does all variables equally and simultaneously, permits us to do just that. Figure 1 shows factor one, the art/technocracy vector, on the horizontal axis, and factor two, technocracy/craft vector on the vertical axis. It displays both individuals and adjectives.

A word of caution about interpretation. In correspondence analysis, it is legitimate to compare clusters of adjectives and to compare, within clusters, their relative positions. Similarly, it is legitimate to compare individuals' positions within and between clusters. As well, it is legitimate to interpret individuals in relation to a group of adjectives. It is not, however, appropriate to speak to one individual and one adjective; that is, we cannot say, "Individual X is *stiff*," because the position of both the individual and the adjective was determined jointly by all the adjectives and all the individuals.

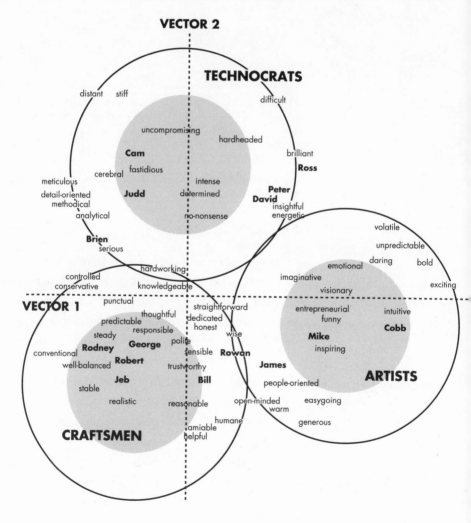

Notes

INTRODUCTION

1 *Le Petit Robert*. Paris: Dictionnaire le Robert, 1990.

2 In Alain-Gérard Slama, *L'Angélisme exterminateur*. Paris: Bernard Grasset, 1993, p. 194.

3 P. E. Trudeau, *Mémoires Politiques*, pp. 217–218. "S'il avait une faiblesse, c'était de manquer d'ordre, d'être souvent brouillon et toujours en train d'improviser . . . lui, me semblait-il, faisait appel aux émotions des Québecois tandis que, de mon côté, je m'efforcais plutôt de leur parler raison." If he [Lévesque] had a weakness it was that he lacked order and was often confused and given to improvisation and to emotional appeals to Quebeckers, whereas I tried to appeal to their logic.

4 Charles Taylor, *Sources of the Self*. Cambridge: Harvard University Press, 1989, p. 512. Charles Taylor is a very "serious" ethical philosopher, but he uses metaphors that resonate, that touch our emotions as much as our intellect, because understanding begins in feeling.

5 Herbert Simon, *The New Science of Management Decision*. New Jersey: Prentice-Hall, 1977.

6 H. Gardner, *The Mind's New Science*. New York: Basic Books, 1985.

7 *Ibid.*, p. 6.

8 M. E. Porter, *Competitive Strategy*, New York: Free Pess, 1980, and *Competitive Advantage*, New York: Free Press, 1985. In a little-noted footnote, Porter admits that his analytic framework can be seen as a substitute for vision (1980:151), but this is a little like saying ball bearings can be a substitute for wheels; they're round but they won't take you very far or very fast.

9 Among others, R. B. Zajonc, "Feeling and Thinking" and "On the Primacy of Affect," appearing in *American Psychologist* in, respectively, 1980 and 1984.

10 A. Isen and K. Daubman, "The Influence of Affect on Categorization," *Journal of Personality and Social Psychology*, 1984, p. 1217.

11 David Shapiro, *Neurotic Styles*. New York: Basic Books, 1965, p. 192.

12 Warren Bennis, *On Becoming a Leader*. New York: Addison-Wesley, 1989. Frances Westley and Henry Mintzberg, "Visionary Leadership and Strategic Management," *Strategic Management Journal*, 1989.

213

13 Herbert Read, *The Origins of Form in Art*. New York: Horizon Press, 1965, p. 88.
14 Michael Polanyi, *Personal Knowledge*. Chicago: University of Chicago Press, 1958, p. 18.
15 S. K. Langer, *Feeling and Form*. New York: Scribner's, 1953, p. 28.
16 Cited in W. O'Flaherty, *Dreams, Illusions and Other Realities*. Chicago: University of Chicago Press, 1984, p. 8.
17 E. Gombrich, *Art and Illusion*. Princeton: Princeton University Press, 1961, pp. 359–60.
18 In J. P. Sartre, *Essays in Existentialism*. New York: Citadel Press, 1965.
19 Fiedler in F. Sparshott, *The Theory of the Arts*. Princeton: Princeton University Press, 1982, p. 626.
20 Lord Brain, *Some Reflections on Genius*. London: Pitman Medical Publishing, 1960.
21 Roger Fry, *Vision and Design*. Harmondsworth: Penguin Books, 1920, p. 29.
22 In V. Tomas (ed.), *Creativity in the Arts*. New Jersey: Prentice-Hall, 1964, p. 47.
23 F. Barron, "Creative Writers," in R. S. Albert (ed.), *Genius and Eminence*. New York: Pergamon Press, 1983, p. 309.
24 In J. Schnier, "The Function and Origin of Form," *Journal of Aesthetics and Art Criticism*, 1957–58, p. 69.
25 In Tomas, p. 40.
26 *Ibid.*, p. 82.
27 In Sparshott, *op. cit.*, p. 623. Emphasis in the original.
28 J. Bronowski, "The Creative Process," *Scientific American*, September 1958.
29 In Sparshott, *op. cit.*, p. 616.
30 In Lord Brain, *op.cit.*, 1960.
31 Jung, C. G., in J. Campbell (ed.), *The Portable Jung*. London: Penguin Books, 1971.
32 S. Arieti, *Creativity: The Magic Synthesis*. New York: Basic Books, 1976. M. Milner, *The Suppressed Madness of Sane Men*. London: Tavistock Publications, 1987. A. Ehrenzweig, *The Hidden Order in Art*. London: Weidenfeld and Nicolson, 1967.
33 Rollo May, *The Courage to Create*. New York: Bantam Books, 1975, p. 62.
34 George Santayana, *Reason in Art*. New York: Dover Publications, 1982, p. 56.
35 Santayana, *Le Petit Robert*.
36 W. Reich, *Character Analysis*. New York: Orgone Institute, 1949, p. 199.
37 Polanyi, *op. cit.*, 1958, p. 240.
38 C. G. Jung, in J. Campbell (ed.), *The Portable Jung*. London: Penguin Books, 1974, p. 314.
39 H. Mintzberg, "Crafting Strategy," *Harvard Business Review*, July–August 1987.
40 In Sparshott, *op. cit.*, 1982, p. 198.
41 H. Osborne, Preface to the *Oxford Companion to Craft*, London: Oxford University Press, 1975, and "The Aesthetic Concept of Craftsmanship," *British Journal of Aesthetics*, spring 1977.
42 Sparshott. *op. cit.*, 1982, p. 131.

43 V. A. Howard, *Artistry: The Work of Artists*. Indiana: Hackett Publishing, 1982, p. 35.

44 Polanyi, *op. cit.*, 1958, p. 53.

45 The details of the organization, names, dates, assets and locations are deliberately vague in order to protect the anonymity of the managers.

46 H. G. Gough, "The Adjective Check List as a Personality Assessment Research Technique," *Psychological Reports*, vol. 6, 1960.

ONE: THE ARTIST

1 Ehrenzweig, *The Hidden Order in Art*. London: Weidenfeld and Nicholson, pp. 50–51. "The third slow movement of the *Hammerclavier Sonata* still startles me by a sudden twist that breaks into the broad beautiful cantilena and produces a melodic as well as an harmonic rupture. The notebooks tell us that it was not the broad adagio theme but this abrupt transition which Beethoven first noted down. How strange: a transition between melodies not yet existing! The melodies unfold later from this rupture between them. Beethoven never revised the break while he kept on filing and refining the broad melodies. Here we have a good example of an inarticulate disruptive idea which *guides* and *unfolds* the large-scale structures."

2 In R. E. M. Harding, *An Anatomy of Inspiration*. New York: Barnes and Noble, 1967, p. 51.

3 A. Georgotas and R. Cancros (eds.), *Depression and Mania*. New York: Elsevier Science Publications, 1988.

4 See P. Rentchnick, *Ces malades qui nous gouvernent*. Paris: Stock, 1976. See also J. J. Schildkraut *et al.*, "Mind and Mood in Modern Art: Depressive Disorders, Spirituality, and Early Deaths in the Abstract Expressionist Artists of the New York School," *The American Journal of Psychiatry*, April 1994.

5 H. Segal in Read, *op. cit.*, p. 62.

6 Cited in F. Westley and H. Mintzberg, "Visionary Leadership and Strategic Management," *Strategic Management Journal*, vol. 10, 1989.

TWO: THE CRAFTSMAN

1 Cited in John Saul, *Voltaire's Bastards*. New York: Penguin Books, 1992, p. 67.

2 H. A. Sackheim, "Self-deception, Self-esteem, and Depression: The Adaptive Value of Lying to Oneself," in J. Masling (ed.), *Empirical Studies of Psychoanalytic Theories*. New Jersey: Earlbaum, 1983.

3 See Laurent Lapierre, "Le Ménagement": ménager, faire le ménage, et se ménager," in *Gestion: Revue Internationale de Gestion*, Nov. 1992. Lapierre does not attribute these attitudes to the Craftsman, but I claim it is the Craftsman that he is describing. He agrees. For the most part, the Artist is not close enough to day-to-day events and people to notice who needs to be disciplined.

THREE: THE TECHNOCRAT

1 There may be more sincere motivations for this interst in art. It may be that art is the one place where, in technocratic eyes, it is legitimate to have feelings. It should go without saying that I am not claiming that all art collectors are Technocrats, but I thought I'd better add this just in case.

2 Goethe, in Schnier, *op. cit.*, p. 98.

3 Platon, *Protagoras.* Paris: Librairie Générale Française, 1993.

4 In technical language, this is "projective identification" — *"He's like me, what a great guy!"* Or "introjective identification" — *"Boy, would I like to be like him."*

5 American Psychiatric Association, *Diagnostic and Statistical Manual of Mental Disorders.* Washington: American Psychiatric Association, 1987.

6 W. G. Dahlstrom, G. S. Welsh and L. E. Dahlstrom, *An MMPI Handbook.* Minneapolis: University of Minnesota Press, 1972, vol. 1, pp. 267–71.

7 *Diagnostic and Statistical Manual of Mental Disorders* (DSM111).

8 See S. Kakar, *Frederick Taylor: A Study in Personality and Innovation.* Cambridge: M.I.T. Press, 1970.

9 David Shapiro, *Neurotic Styles.* New York: Basic Books, 1965, p. 192.

10 L. Hinsie and R. J. Campbell, *Psychiatric Dictionary.* London: Oxford University Press, 1970, p. 105.

FIVE: THE DREAMS OF THE PLAYWRIGHT

1 Baltimore: Johns Hopkins University Press, 1967, vol. 1, p. 90.

SEVEN: CLIMAX: THE TRIUMPH OF TECHNICAL ILLUSIONS

1 Alleged report of a work-study engineer circulating in the U.K. in the 1950s and cited in William J. Baumol and William G. Bowen, *Performing Arts — The Economic Dilemma.* Cambridge: M.I.T. Press, 1966, p. 165.

EIGHT: DÉNOUEMENT: THE COLLAPSE OF VISION

1 *The Sources of the Self: The Making of the Modern Identity, ibid.*, p. 24.

2 This "strategic" approach to human relations is characteristic of the paranoid personality: assuming that others are plotting against him, he adopts what seems to him to be a legitimate defensive strategy against them.

3 From *sophist*: paid teacher of philosophy in ancient Greece; reasoner willing to avail himself of fallacies that will help his case. *Sophism*: a false argument meant to deceive; *sophisticate*: spoil the simplicity or purity or naturalness of, corrupt or adulterate or tamper with.

4 Barbara Tuschman, *A Distant Mirror.* New York: Alfred Knopf, 1978.

NINE: LEADERSHIP REVISITED

1 "Managers and Leaders: Are They Different?" *Harvard Business Review*, May–June 1977.
2 *The Managerial Mystique*. New York: Harper and Row, 1989.
3 The Book of Job, *The Bible*.
4 Alain-Gérard Slama, *L'Angélisme exterminateur*. Paris: Bernard Grasset, 1993.

TEN: WHAT DO ORGANIZATIONS NEED?

1 Preface to Otto Rank, *Art and Artist*. New York: Alfred Knopf, 1932.
2 J. B. Quinn, "Strategic Change: Logical Incrementalism," *Sloan Management Review*, fall 1978.
3 *Le Big Bang des Organisations*. Paris: Calmann-Lévy, 1993.
4 *La Presse*, Feb. 12, 1994.
5 Laurent Lapierre, "Diriger ou pas Diriger: Voilà la question!" *Gestion: Revue Internationale de Gestion*, vol. 16, no. 4, Nov. 1991, pp. 54-55.
6 R. Giuliani, "Freedom Is About Authority," *New York Times*, March 20, 1994.
7 S. Arieti, *Creativity*.
8 *English Etymology*. London: Oxford University Press, 1993, p. 79.
9 A. Glassman, "Cigarette Smoking: Implications for Psychiatric Illness," *American Journal of Psychiatry*, April 1993.

ELEVEN: NOTES ON EDUCATION

1 Alain-Gérard Slama, *L'Angélisme exterminateur*. Paris: Bernard Grasset, 1993.
2 Camille Paglia, *Sex, Art and American Culture*. New York: Vintage Books, 1992.
3 H. Margolis, *Patterns, Thinking and Cognition*. Chicago: University of Chicago Press, 1987, p. 229.
4 See Alain Chanlat, *Gestion et culture d'enterprise*. Montreal: Québec/Amérique, 1984.
5 "Every age has its own outlook. It is specially good at seeing certain truths and specially liable to make certain mistakes. We all, therefore, need the books that will correct the characteristic mistakes of our own period. And that means the old books." C. S. Lewis, "On the Reading of Old Books," in *First and Second Things*. London: Collins and Sons, 1985, p. 27.
6 Robertson Davies, *The Rebel Angels*. New York: Penguin Books, 1981, p. 186.

TWELVE: AN ODE TO CRAFTSMANSHIP

1 T. S. Eliot, *Choruses from the "Rock."*

THIRTEEN: SOME SOCIAL AND ECONOMIC IMPLICATIONS

1 Author's translation of excerpt from Michel Albert, *Capitalisme contre Capitalisme*. Paris: Editions du Seuil, 1991, p. 55.

2 Heinz C. Hoppe, *Serving the Star Around the World*. Munich: Südwest-Verlag, 1992, p. 105.

3 Albert, op. cit., p. 137.

FOURTEEN: BABY BOOMERS: ON "COCOONING"

1 Hosea 8:7, *The Bible*.

Bibliography

Abelson, R. (1981) "Psychological Status of the Script Concept," *American Psychologist*, vol. 36.

Aktouf, O. (1987) *Methodologie des sciences sociales et approche Qualitative des Organisations*. Québec: Université de Québec.

Albert, M. (1991) *Capitalisme contre Capitalisme*. Paris: Editions du Seuil.

Albert, R. S. (ed.) (1983) *Genius and Eminence*. New York: Pergamon Press.

Aldrich, H. (1979) *Organizations and Environments*. New Jersey: Prentice-Hall.

Allison, G. (1971) *Essence of Decision: Explaining the Cuban Missile Crisis*. Boston: Little Brown.

American Psychiatric Association (1987) *Diagnostic and Statistical Manual of Mental Disorders*. Third edition, revised. Washington: American Psychiatric Association.

Anderson, H. (1987) "Why Artificial Intelligence Isn't (Yet)," *A I Expert*, July.

Andrews, K. (1980) *The Concept of Corporate Strategy*. Homewood, Ill.: Richard Irwin.

Ansoff, I. (1965) *Corporate Strategy*. New York: McGraw-Hill.

Arieti, S. (1976) *Creativity: The Magic Synthesis*. New York: Basic Books.

Baliga, B. R. and A. Jaeger (1987) "Blinded by the Scripts: A Cognitive Sciences Perspective of Strategic Management." Montreal: McGill University.

Barnes, Jr., J. (1984) "Cognitive Biases and Their Impact on Stategic Planning," *Strategic Management Journal*, vol. 5.

Barrett, W. (1986) *The Death of the Soul*. New York: Anchor Books.

Barron, F. (1983) "Creative Writers" in R. S. Albert (ed.) *Genius and Eminence*. New York: Pergamon Press.

Bartlett, F. C. (1932) *Remembering*. Cambridge: Cambridge University Press.

Bennis, W. (1989) *On Becoming a Leader*. New York: Addison-Wesley.

Benzecri, J. P. *et al.* (1979) *L'Analyse des Correspondences*, vol. 2. Paris: Dunod.

Berg, N. (1984) *General Management: An Analytic Approach*. Homewood, Ill.: Richard Irwin.

Bourgon, M. G. (1983) "Uncovering Cognitive Maps" in G. Morgan (ed.) *Beyond Method*. Beverly Hills: Sage Publications.

Bowen, M. (1987) "The Escalation Phenomenon Reconsidered: Decision Dilemmas or Decision Errors," *Academy of Management Review*, vol. 12, no. 1.

219

Bower, G. H. (1981) "Mood and Memory," *American Psychologist*, Feb., vol. 36, no. 2.

Bowman, E. H. (1974) "Epistemology, Corporate Strategy, and Academe," *Sloan Management Review*, winter.

Brain, Lord R. (1960) *Some Reflections on Genius*. London: Pitman Medical Publishing.

Brain, Lord R. (1963) "Diagnosis of Genius," *British Journal of Aesthetics*.

Bronowski, J. (1978) *The Origins of Knowledge and Imagination*. New Haven: Yale University Press.

Bronowski, J. (1958) "The Creative Process," *Scientific American*, Sept.

Brooks, L. (1978) "Non-Analytic Concept Formation and Memory for Instances" in E. Rosch and B. Lloyd (eds.) *Cognition and Categorization*. New Jersey: Earlbaum.

Bruner, J., J. Goodnow and J. Austin (1956) *A Study of Thinking*. New York: John Wiley & Sons.

Brunsson, N. (1985) *The Irrational Organization*. New York: John Wiley and Sons.

Cattell, R. B. (1983) "The Processes of Creative Thought" in R. Albert (ed.) *Genius and Eminence*. New York: Pergamon Press.

Challem, J. J. (1978) "Casual Notes on Creativity and Schizophrenia," *Orthomolecular Psychiatry*, vol. 7, no. 1.

Chandler, A. (1962) *Strategy and Structure: Chapters in the History of the Industrial Enterprise*. Cambridge: M.I.T. Press.

Chanlat, A. (1984) *Gestion et culture d'enterprise*. Montreal: Québec/Amérique.

Chatman, J., N. Bell and B. Staw (1986) "The Managed Thought: The Role of Self Justification and Impression Management in Organizational Settings" in H. Sims Jr. and D. Gioia (eds.) *The Thinking Organization*. San Francisco: Jossey-Bass.

Child, J. (1972) "Organizational Structure, Environment and Performance: The Role of Strategic Choice," *Sociology*, Jan.

Christensen R. *et al.* (1987) *Business Policy: Text and Cases*. Homewood, Ill.: Richard Irwin.

Clausewitz, Carl (1968) *On War*. London: Penguin Books.

Cohen, J. and K. Basu (1987) "Alternative Models of Categorization: Toward a Contingent Processing Framework," *Journal of Consumer Research*, vol. 13, March.

Cohen, L. J. (1981) "Can Human Irrationality Be Experimentally Demonstrated?" *Behavioral and Brain Sciences*, vol. 4.

Collingwood, R. G. (1938) *The Principles of Art*. London: Oxford University Press.

Collins, O. and D. G. Moore (1970) *The Organization Makers*. New York: Appleton-Century-Crofts.

Cyert, R. and J. March (1963) *A Behavioral Theory of the Firm*. New Jersey: Prentice-Hall.

Daft, R. and K. Weick (1984) "Toward a Model of Organizations as Interpretation Systems," *Academy of Management Review*, vol. 9, no. 2.

Dahlstrom, W. G., G. S. Welsh and L. E. Dahlstrom (1972) *An MMPI Handbook*, vols. 1 and 2. Minneapolis: University of Minnesota Press.

Daniel, D. W. (1979) "What Influences a Decision? Some Results from a Highly Controlled Defence Game," *Omega: The International Journal of Management Science*, vol. 8, no. 4.

Davies, R. (1981) *The Rebel Angels*. New York: Penguin Books.

DeBono, E. (1970) *Lateral Thinking*. Harmondsworth: Penguin Books.

Devereux, G. (1980) *De l'Angoisse à la methode dans les sciences du comportement*. Paris: Flammarion.

Downey, H. and A. Brief (1986) "How Cognitive Structures Affect Organizational Design: Implicit Theories of Organizing" in H. Sims Jr. and D. Gioia (eds.) *The Thinking Organization*. San Francisco: Jossey-Bass.

Drucker, P. (1959) "Long-range Planning," *Management Science*, vol. 5, April.

Duhaime, I. M. and C. Schwenk (1985) "Cognitive Simplification Processes in Acquisition and Divestment Decision-Making," *Academy of Management Review*, vol. 10.

Dutton, J. and S. Jackson (1987) "Categorizing Strategic Issues: Links to Organizational Action," *Academy of Management Review*, vol. 12, no. 1.

Dutton, J., L. Fahey and V. K. Narayanan (1983) "Towards Understanding Strategic Issue Diagnosis," *Strategic Management Journal*, vol. 4.

Eaton, M. (1983) *Art and Non-Art*. London: Associated University Presses.

Eden, C. and S. Jones (1984) "Using Repertory Grids for Problem Construction," *Journal of the Operational Research Society*, vol. 35, no. 9.

Ehrenzweig, A. (1967) *The Hidden Order in Art*. London: Weidenfeld and Nicolson.

Fahey, L. and V. K. Narayanan (1987) "Linking Changes in Cognitive Maps, the Environment, and the Top Management Team: An Empirical Study." Paper presented at the workshop on Managerial Thinking in Business Environments, Boston, Oct. 13.

Feldman, J. (1986) "On the Difficulty of Learning from Experience" in H. Sims Jr. and D. Gioia (eds.) *The Thinking Organization*. San Francisco: Jossey-Bass.

Fenelon, J.-P. (1981) *Qu'est-ce que c'est l'analyse des données?* Paris: Lefonen.

Freud, S. (1977) *Inhibitions, Symptoms and Anxiety*, James Strachey, ed. New York: Norton.

Freud, S. (1979) *Case Histories II*, A. Richards, ed. London: Penguin Books.

Fry, R. (1920) *Vision and Design*. Harmondsworth: Penguin Books.

Fuller, C., J. Porac and H. Thomas (1987) "Taxonomic Cognitive Structures in the U.K. Knitwear Industry." Paper presented at the workshop on Managerial Thinking in Business Environments, Boston, Oct. 13.

Gardner, H. (1985) *The Mind's New Science*. New York: Basic Books.

Georgotas, A. and R. Cancro (eds.) (1988) *Depression and Mania*. New York: Elsevier Science Publishing.

Getzels, J. and M. Csikszentmihalyi (1976) *The Creative Vision: A Longitudinal Study of Problem Finding in Art*. New York: John Wiley and Sons.

Ghiselin, B. (1952) *The Creative Process*. Berkeley: University of California Press.

Gilberstadt, H. and J. Duker (1965) *A Handbook for Clinical and Actuarial MMPI Interpretation*. Philadelphia: W.B. Saunders.

Gilligan, S. and G. H. Bower (1984) "Cognitive Consequences of Emotional Arousal" in C. Izard, J. Kagan and R. Zajonc (eds.) *Emotions, Cognition, and Behavior*. Cambridge: Cambridge University Press.

Gilmore and Brandenberg (1962) "Anatomy of Corporate Planning," *Harvard Business Review*, vol. 40, Dec.

Gioia, D. and P. Poole (1984) "Scripts in Organizational Behavior," *Academy of Management Review*, vol. 9, no. 3.

Glaser, B. and A. Strauss (1967) *The Discovery of Grounded Theory: Strategies for Qualitative Research*. Aldine Press.

Gombrich, E. H. (1961) *Art and Illusion*. Princeton: Princeton University Press.

Goodman, N. (1984) *Of Mind and Other Matters*. Cambridge: Harvard University Press.

Gough, H. G. (1960) "The Adjective Checklist as a Personality Assessment Research Technique," *Psychological Reports*, vol. 6.

Govindarajan V. (1989) "Implementing Competitive Strategy at the Business Unit Level: Implications of Matching Managers to Strategies," *Strategic Management Journal*, vol. 10, no. 3.

Grinyer, P. H. and J.-C. Spender (1979) *Turnaround: Managerial Recipes for Strategic Success: The Fall and Rise of the Newton Chambers Group*. London: Associated Business Press.

Guilford, J. P. (1950) "Creativity," *American Psychologist*, vol. 5.

Gupta, A. (1984) "Contingency Linkages between Strategy and General Manager Characteristics: A Conceptual Examination," *Academy of Management Review*, vol. 9, no. 3.

Guth, W. and A. Ginsberg (1990) "Guest Editors' Introduction: Corporate Entrepreneurship," *Strategic Management Journal*, vol. 11.

Guth, W. and R. Tagiuri (1965) "Personal Values and Corporate Strategy," *Harvard Business Review*, Sept.–Oct.

Hambrick, D. C. (1981) "Strategic Awareness with Top Management Teams," *Strategic Management Journal*, vol. 2.

Hambrick, D. C. (1989) "Guest Editor's Introduction: Putting Managers Back in the Strategy Picture," *Strategic Management Journal*, vol. 10.

Hambrick, D. C. and P. Mason (1984) "Upper Echelons: The Organization as a Reflection of its Top Managers," *Academy of Management Review*, vol. 9, no. 2.

Harding, R. E. M. (1967) *An Anatomy of Inspiration*. New York: Barnes and Noble.

Hedberg, B., and S. Jonsson (1977) "Strategy Formulation as a Discontinuous Process," *International Studies of Management and Organization*.

Hill, W. and C. Granger (1956) "Long-range Planning for Company Growth," *The Management Review*, Dec.

Hinsie, L. and R. J. Campbell (1970) *Psychiatric Dictionary*. London: Oxford University Press.

Hodgkinson, G. and G. Johnson (1987) "Exploring the Mental Models of Competitive Strategists: The Case for Processual Approach." Paper presented at the workshop on Managerial Thinking in Business Environments, Boston, Oct. 13.

Hogarth, R. M. and S. Makridakis (1981) "Forecasting and Planning: An Evaluation," *Management Science*, vol. 27, no. 2, Feb.

Howard, V. A. (1982) *Artistry: The Work of Artists*. Indiana: Hackett Publishing.

Huff, A. (1980) "Evocative Metaphors," *Human Systems Management*, Nov.

Huff, A. (1982) "Industry Influences on Strategy Reformulation," *Strategic Management Journal*, vol. 3.

Hurst, D. K., J. C. Rush and R. E. White (1989) "Top Management Teams and Organizational Renewal," *Strategic Management Journal*, vol. 10.

Hurst, D. K. (1986) "Why Strategic Management Is Bankrupt," *Organizational Dynamics*, autumn.

Isen, A. and K. Daubman (1984) "The Influence of Affect on Categorization" in *Journal of Personality and Social Psychology*, vol. 47, no. 6.

Jackson, S. and J. Dutton (1988) "Discerning Threats and Opportunities." Unpublished, New York University.

Jacoby, L. and L. Brooks (1984) "Non-Analytic Cognition: Memory, Perception and Concept Learning," *The Psychology of Learning and Motivation*, vol. 18.

Jardim, A. (1970) *The First Henry Ford: A Study in Personality*, Cambridge: M.I.T. Press.

Johnston, P. (1989a) "Batteries Not Included: The Cognitive Perspective in Strategic Management." Montreal: McGill University.

Johnston, P. (1989b) "Strategy in the Artistic Mode." Montreal: McGill University.

Jonsson, S., R. Lundin and L. Sjoberg (1977–8) "Frustration in Decision Processes: A Tentative Frame of Reference," *ISMO*, fall-winter.

Jung, C. G. (1971) in J. Campbell (ed.) *The Portable Jung*. London: Penguin Books.

Kaelin, E. (1970) *Art and Existence: A Phenomenological Aesthetics*. Lewisburg: Bucknell University Press.

Kahneman, D., P. Slovic and A. Tversky (eds.) (1982) *Judgement under Uncertainty: Heuristic and Biases*. Cambridge: Cambridge University Press.

Kakar, S. (1970) *Frederick Taylor: A Study in Personality and Innovation*. Cambridge: M.I.T. Press.

Kerlinger, F. (1986) *Foundations of Behavioural Research*. New York: Holt, Rhinehart and Winston.

Kets De Vries, M. (1977) "The Entrepreneurial Personality: A Person at the Crossroads," *Journal of Management Studies*, vol. 14.

Kets de Vries, M. (1980) *Organizational Paradoxes*. London: Tavistock Publications.

Kets de Vries, M. and D. Miller (1984) *The Neurotic Organization*. San Francisco: Jossey-Bass.

Kets de Vries, M. (ed.) (1984) *The Irrational Executive*. New York: International University Press.

Kets de Vries, M. (1989) *Prisoners of Leadership*. New York: John Wiley and Sons.

Kets de Vries, M. F. R. and D. Miller (1989) *Unstable at the Top*. New York: New American Library.

Kavanagh, R. (1990) *The Art of Earth and Fire*. Ph.D. dissertation. Montreal: Concordia University.

Khandwalla, P. (1976–7) "Some Top Management Styles, Their Context and Performance," *Organization and Administrative Sciences*, vol. 7, no. 4.

Kiesler, S. and L. Sproull (1982) "Managerial Response to Changing Environments: Perspectives on Problem-Sensing from Social Cognition," *Administrative Science Quarterly*, vol. 27.

Klein, M. (1935) "A Contribution to the Psychogenesis of Manic-Depressive States" in J. Mitchell (ed.) *The Selected Melanie Klein*. London: Penguin Books, 1986.

Klein, M. (1940) "Infantile Anxiety Situations Reflected in a Work of Art and in the Creative Impulse" in J. Mitchell (ed.) *The Selected Melanie Klein*. London: Penguin Books, 1986.

Klein, M. (1940) "Mourning and its Relation to Manic-Depressive States" in J. Mitchell (ed.) *The Selected Melanie Klein*. London: Penguin Books, 1986.

Koestler, A. (1979) *Janus: A Summing Up*. London: Pan Books.

Kris, E. (1952) *Psychoanalytic Explorations in Art*. New York: International Universities Press.

Kuhn, T. (1962) *The Structure of Scientific Revolutions*. Chicago: Chicago University Press.

Lalonde, P. and F. Grunberg *et al.* (1988) *Psychiatrie clinique: approche bio-psycho-sociale*. Montreal: Gaetan Morin.

Langer, S. K. (1967) *Mind: An Essay on Human Feeling*. Baltimore: Johns Hopkins University Press, vols. 1–3.

Langer, S. K. *Feeling and Form*. New York: Charles Scribner, 1953.

Lapierre, L. (1984) *Le(La) Metteur(e) en scene de théâtre: un(e) gestionnaire*. PhD dissertation. Montreal: McGill University.

Lapierre, L. (1989) "Mourning, Potency, and Power in Management," *Human Relations*, vol. 28.

Lapierre, L. (1991) " Diriger ou pas Diriger: Voilà la question!", vol. 16, no. 4, Nov., pp. 54-55.

Lapierre, L. (1992) "'Le Ménagement': ménger, faire le ménage, et se ménager," *Gestion: Revue Internationale de Gestion*, Nov.

Lawrence, B. S. (1984) "Historical Perspective: Using the Past to Study the Present," *Academy of Management Review*, vol. 9, no. 2.

Lebart, L., A. Morineau and K. M. Warwick (1984) *Multivariate Descriptive Statistical Analysis*. New York: John Wiley and Sons.

Leontiades, M. (1982) "Choosing the Right Manager to Fit the Strategy," *Journal of Business Strategy*, vol. 3, no. 2.

Levitt, T. (1960) "Marketing Myopia," *Harvard Business Review*, July-Aug.

Lewis, C. S. (1985) "On the Reading of Old Books" in *First and Second Things*. London: Collins and Sons.

Lewisohn, L. (1932) "Preface" in Otto Rank, *Art and Artist*. New York: Alfred Knopf.

Lieberson, S. and J. F. O'Connor (1972) "Leadership and Organizational Performance: A Study of Large Corporations," *American Sociological Review*, vol. 37.

Lindblom, C. E. (1959) "The Science of Muddling Through," *Public Administration Review*.

Livingston, J. (1971) "The Myth of the Well-educated Manager," *Harvard Business Review*, Jan.

Lyles, M. (1981) "Formulating Strategic Problems: Empirical Analysis and Model Development," *Strategic Management Journal*, vol. 2.

Maccoby, M. (1976) *The Gamesman*. New York: Simon and Schuster.

Macquarrie, J. (1972) *Existentialism*. London: Penguin Books.

March, J. (1978) "Bounded Rationality, Ambiguity and the Engineering of Choice," *Bell Journal of Economics*, vol. 9.

Marcuse, L. (1958) "Freud's Aesthetics," *Journal of Aesthetics and Art Criticism*, vol. 17.

Margolis, H. (1987) *Patterns, Thinking, and Cognition*. Chicago: University of Chicago Press.

May, R. (1975) *The Courage to Create*. New York: Bantam Books.

May, R. (1983) *The Discovery of Being*. London: W. W. Norton.

Mayer, R. (1977) *Thinking and Problem-Solving*. Glenview: Scott, Foresman.

McDougall, J. (1978) *Plaidoyer pour une certaine anormalité*. Paris: Gallimard.

McMillan, J. and S. Schumacher (1984) "Analytical Research: Historical, Legal, and Policy Studies," *Reseach in Education: A Conceptual Introduction*. Boston: Little Brown.

Medin, D. and M. Schaffer (1978) "Context Theory of Classification Learning," *Psychological Review*, vol. 85, no. 3.

Meindl, J. R. and S. B. Ehrlichman (1987) "The Romance of Leadership and the Evolution of Corporate Performance," *Academy of Management Journal*, vol. 30, no. 1.

Meindl, J. R., S. B. Ehrlichman and J. M. Dukerich (1985) "The Romance of Leadership," *Administrative Science Quarterly*, vol. 30.

Michel, J. G. and D. Hambrick (1992) "Diversification Posture and Top Management Team Characteristics," *Academy of Management Journal*, vol. 35, no. 1.

Miller, D. and P. Friesen (1980) "Archetypes of Organizational Transition," *Administrative Science Quarterly*, vol. 25, June.

Miller, D. and C. Dröge (1986) "Psychological and Traditional Determinants of Structure," *Administrative Science Quarterly*, Dec.

Miller, D., M. Kets de Vries and J. M. Toulouse (1982) "Top Executive Locus of Control and Its Relationship to Strategy-making, Structure and Environment," *Academy of Management Journal*, vol. 25.

Miller, G. A. (1978) "Practical and Lexical Knowledge" in E. Rosch and B. Lloyd (eds.) *Cognition and Categorization*. New Jersey: Earlbaum.

Miller, G. A. and P. Johnson-Laird (1976) *Language and Perception*. Cambridge: The Belknap Press of Harvard University Press.

Milner, M. (1987) *The Suppressed Madness of Sane Men*. London: Tavistock Publications.

Minsky, M. (1975) "A Framework for Representing Knowledge" in P. H. Winston (ed.) *The Psychology of Computer Vision*. New York: McGraw-Hill.

Mintzberg, H. (1973) "Strategy Making in Three Modes," *California Management Review*, vol. 16, no. 2.

Mintzberg, H. (1979) "Beyond Implementation" in K. B. Haley (ed.) *OR '78*. North Holland.

Mintzberg, H. (1983) *Structure in Fives*. New Jersey: Prenctice-Hall.

Mintzberg, H. and J. Waters (1985) "Of Strategies Deliberate and Emergent," *Strategic Management Journal*, vol. 6.

Mintzberg, H. and J. Waters (1984) "Researching the Formation of Strategies: The History of Canadian Lady, 1939–1976" in R. B. Lamb (ed.) *Corporate Strategic Management*. New Jersey: Prentice-Hall.

Mintzberg, H. (1987) "Crafting Strategy," *Harvard Business Review*, July–Aug.

Mitrof, I. and R. Mason (1980) "A Logic for Strategic Management," *Human Systems Management*, vol. 1.

Mitrof, I. and S. Mohrman (1987) "Correcting Tunnel Vision," *Journal of Business Strategy*, winter.

Morgan, G. and L. Smircich (1980) "The Case for Qualitative Research," *Academy of Management Review*, vol. 4.

Mullen, T. and S. Stumph (1987) "The Effect of Management Styles on Strategic Planning," *Journal of Business Strategy*, vol. 7, no. 3.

Murphy, G. and D. Medin (1985) "The Role of Theories in Conceptual Coherence," *Psychological Review*, vol. 92, no. 3, July.

Naumburg, M. (1955) "Art as Symbolic Speech," *Journal of Aesthetics and Art Criticism*, vol. 13.

Neisser, U. (1976) *Cognition and Reality*. New York: Freeman.

Nisbett, R. and L. Ross (1980) *Human Inference: Strategies and Shortcomings of Social Judgment*. New Jersey: Prenctice-Hall.

O'Flaherty, W. (1984) *Dreams, Illusions and Other Realities*. Chicago: University of Chicago Press.

Osborn, A. F. (1953) *Applied Imagination*. New York: Scribners.

Osborne, H. (1975) "Preface," *The Oxford Companion to Craft*. London: Oxford University Press.

Osborne, H. (1977) "The Aesthetic Concept of Craftsmanship," *British Journal of Aesthetics*, vol. 17, spring.

Overall, J. E. and C. J. Klett (1972) *Applied Multivariate Analysis*. New York: McGraw-Hill.

Oxford English Dictionary. (1933) Oxford: Clarendon Press.

Park, Oh Soo, H. Sims, Jr. and S. J. Motowidlo (1986) "Affect in Organizations: How Feelings and Emotions Influence Managerial Judgement" in H. Sims Jr. and D. Gioia (eds.) *The Thinking Organization*. San Francisco: Jossey-Bass.

Patton, M. Q. (1982) "Qualitative Methods and Approaches: What Are They?" in E. Kuhns and S. V. Marorana (eds.) *Qualitative Methods for Institutional Research*. San Francisco: Jossey-Bass.

Le Petit Robert (1990) Paris: Dictionnaires le Robert.

Pfeffer, J. and G. Salancik (1978) *The External Control of Organizations: A Resource Dependence Perspective*. New York: Harper and Row.

Philipson, M. (1963) *Outline of a Jungian Aesthetics*. Evanston: Northwestern University Press.

Platon (1993) *Protagoras*. Paris: Librairie Générale Française.

Polanyi, M. (1958) *Personal Knowledge*. Chicago: University of Chicago Press.

Polanyi, M. (1959) *The Study of Man*. Chicago: University of Chicago Press.

Porac, J., H. Thomas and B. Emme (1987) "Knowing the Competition: The Mental Models of Retailing Strategists" in G. Johnson (ed.) *Business Strategy and Retailing*. London: John Wiley and Sons.

Porter, M. E. (1980) *Competitive Strategy*. New York: Free Press.

Porter, M. E. (1985) *Competitive Advantage*. New York: Free Press.

Quinn, J. B. (1978) "Strategic Change: Logical Incrementalism," *Sloan Management Review*, fall.

Quinn, J. B. (1980) "Managing Strategic Change," *Sloan Management Review*, summer.

Quinn, J. B. (1980) *Strategies for Change: Logical Incrementalism*. Homewood, Ill.: Richard Irwin.

Read, H. (1965) *The Origins of Form in Art*. New York: Horizon Press.

Read, S. (1983) "Once Is Enough: Causal Reasoning from a Single Instance," *Journal of Personality and Social Psychology*, vol. 45, no. 2.

Reich, W. (1933) *Character Analysis*. New York: Orgone Institute Press.

Reilly, E. (1955) "Planning the Strategy of the Business," *Advanced Management*, Dec.

Rentchnick, P. (1976) *Ces malades qui nous gouvernent*. Paris: Stock.

Rosche, E. (1978) "Principles of Categorization" in E. Rosch and B. Lloyd (eds.) *Cognition and Categorization*. New Jersey: Earlbaum.

Rosche, E. and C. B. Mervis (1975) "Family Resemblances: Studies in the Internal Structure of Categories," *Cognitive Psychology*, vol. 7.

Ross, L., M. Lepper and M. Hubbard (1975) "Perseverance in Self-perception and Social Perception: Biased Attributional Processes in the De-briefing Paradigm," *Journal of Personality and Social Psychology*, vol. 32.

Rossman, J. (1931) *The Psychology of the Inventor*. Washington: Inventors Publishing.

Rumelt, R. (1979) "Evaluation of Strategy: Theory and Models" in Schendel and Hofer (eds.) *Strategic Management*. Boston: Little Brown.

Sachs, Hanns (1951) *The Creative Unconscious: Studies in the Psychoanalysis of Art*. Cambridge, Mass.: Sci-Art Publications.

Sackheim, H. A. (1983) "Self-Deception, Self-Esteem, and Depression: The Adaptive Value of Lying to Oneself" in J. Masling (ed.) *Empirical Studies of Psychoanalytic Theories*. New Jersey: Earlbaum.

Salancik, G. and J. Porac (1986) "Distilled Ideologies: Values Derived from Causal Reasoning in Complex Environments" in H. Sims, Jr. and D. Gioia (eds.) *The Thinking Organization*. San Francisco: Jossey-Bass.

Santayana, G. (1982) *Reason in Art*. New York: Dover Publications.

Sartre, J. P. (1965) *Essays in Existentialism*. New York: Citadel Press.

Schank, R. C. and R. P. Abelson (1977) *Scripts, Plans, Goals, and Understanding*. New Jersey: Earlbaum.

Schendel, D. (1989) "Introduction to the Second Special Issue," *Strategic Management Journal*, vol. 10.

Schildkraut, J. J. *et al.* (1994) "Mind and Mood in Modern Art: Depressive Disorders, Spirituality, and Early Deaths in the Abstract Expressionist Artists of the New York School," *The American Journal of Psychiatry*, April.

Schneider, S. and R. Angelmar (1988) "Cognition and Organizational Analysis: Who's Minding the Store?" Working paper, INSEAD, France.

Schnier, K. (1957–8) "The Function and Origin of Form," *Journal of Aesthetics and Art Criticism*, vol. 16.

Schwenk, C. (1984) "Cognitive Simplification Processes in Strategic Decision-Making," *Strategic Management Journal*, vol. 5.

Schwenk, C. (1988) "The Cognitive Perspective on Strategic Decision-making," *Journal of Management Studies*, vol. 25, no. 1, Jan.

Sérieyx, H. (1993) *Le Big Bang des Organisations*. Paris: Calmann-Lévy.

Shapiro, D. (1965) *Neurotic Styles*. New York: Basic Books.

Simon, H. (1977) *The New Science of Management Decision*. New Jersey: Prentice-Hall.

Simon, H. and G. Chase (1979) "Perception in Chess" in H. Simon (ed.) *Models of Thought*. New Haven: Yale University Press.

Slama, A.-G. (1993) *L'Angélisme exterminateur*. Paris: Bernard Grasset.

Smith, E. E. and D. Medin (1981) *Categories and Concepts*. Cambridge: Harvard University Press.

Smith, J. and D. Kemler Nelson (1984) "Overall Similarity in Adults' Classification: The Child in All of Us," *Journal of Experimental Psychology: General*, vol. 113, no. 1.

Soelberg (1967) "Unprogrammed Decision Making," *Industrial Management Review*, spring.

Sparshott, F. (1982) *The Theory of the Arts*. Princeton: Princeton University Press.

Staw, B. M. (1976) "Knee-Deep in the Big Muddy: A Study of Escalating Commitment to a Chosen Course of Action," *Organizational Behavior and Human Performance*, vol. 16.

Staw, B. M. and J. Ross (1978) "Commitment to a Policy Decision: A Multi-Theoretical Perspective," *Administrative Science Quarterly* vol. 23, March.

Steinbruner, J. (1974) *The Cybernetic Theory of Decision: New Dimensions of Political Analysis*. Princeton: Princeton University Press.

Stokes, A. (1959–60) "Form in Art: A Psychoanalytic Interpretation," *Journal of Aesthetics and Art Criticism*, vol. 18.

Szilagyi, Jr., A. D. and D. M. Schweiger (1984) "Matching Managers to Strategies: A Review and Suggested Framework," *Academy of Management Review*, vol. 9, no. 4.

Taylor, C. (1989) *The Sources of the Self*. Cambridge: Harvard University Press.

Taylor, S. E. and J. Crocker (1981) "Schematic Bases of Social Information Processing" in E. Tory Higgins, C. A. Hannan and M. P. Zanna (eds.) *Social Cognition: The Ontario Symposium on Personality and Social Psychology*. New Jersey: Earlbaum.

Thomas, A. B. (1988) "Does Leadership Make a Difference to Organizational Performance?" *Administrative Science Quarterly*, vol. 30.

Thomas, H. (1984) "Mapping Strategic Research," *Journal of General Management*, vol. 9.

Thompson, J. D. (1967) *Organizations in Action*. New York: McGraw-Hill.

Tilles (1963) "How to Evaluate Corporate Strategy," *Harvard Business Review*, vol. 41, July.

Tolman, E. C. (1948) "Cognitive Maps in Rats and Men," *Psychological Review*, vol. 55.

Tomas, V. (ed.) (1964) *Creativity in the Arts*. New Jersey: Prentice-Hall.

Tuschman, B. (1978) *A Distant Mirror*. New York: Knopf.

Tversky, A. and D. Kahneman (1981) "The Framing of Decisions and the Psychology of Choice," *Science*, vol. 211, Jan.

Uyterhoeven H., R. Ackermen and J. Rosenblum (1977) *Strategy and Organization.* Homewood: Ill.: Richard Irwin.

Vincent, K. *et al.* (1984) *MMPI–168 Codebook.* New Jersey: Ablex Publishing.

Waelder, R. (1965) "Motivation and Resolution" in J. Hogg (ed.) *Psychology and the Visual Arts.* Middlesex: Penguin Books.

Wallas, G. (1926) *The Art of Thought.* New York: Harcourt, Brace.

Walsh, J. (1988) "Approaches to the Study of Cognition in Organizations." Unpublished, Amos Tuck School of Business Administration, Hanover, N.H., July.

Walton, E. (1986) "Managers' Prototypes of Financial Firms," *Journal of Management Studies,* vol. 23, no. 6, Nov.

Weick, K. and M. Bourgon (1986) "Organizations as Cognitive Maps: Charting Ways to Success and Failure, in Organizational Settings" in H. Sims Jr. and D. Gioia (eds.) *The Thinking Organization.* San Francisco: Jossey-Bass.

Weick, K. (1979) *The Social Psychology of Organizing.* New York: Random House.

Weitz, M. (1956) "The Role of Theory in Aesthetics," *Journal of Aesthetics and Art Criticism,* vol. 15.

Welsh, G. S. and W. G. Dahlstrom (eds.) (1956) *Basic Readings on the MMPI in Psychology and Medicine.* Minneapolis: University of Minnesota Press.

Welsh, G. S. (1959) *Welsh Figure Preference Test.* Palo Alto: Consulting Psychologists Press.

Wertheimer, M. (1945) *Productive Thinking.* New York: Harper and Row.

Wessema, J. G., H. W. Van der Pol and H. M. Messer (1980) "Strategic Management Archetypes," *Strategic Management Journal,* vol. 1.

Westley, F. and H. Mintzberg (1989) "Visionary Leadership and Strategic Management," *Strategic Management Journal,* vol. 10.

Whyte, G. (1986) "Escalating Commitment to a Course of Action: A Re-Interpretation," *Academy of Management Review,* vol. 11, no. 2.

Wiggins, J. S. (1973) *Personality and Prediction: Principles of Personality Assessment.* Reading: Addison-Wesley.

Winner, E. (1982) *Invented Worlds: The Psychology of the Arts.* Cambridge: Harvard University Press.

Winograd, T. (1980) "What Does it Mean to Understand Language," *Cognitive Science,* vol. 4.

Wittgenstein, L. (1968) *Philosophical Investigations.* New York: Macmillan.

Wrapp, H. (1967) "Good Managers Don't Make Policy Decisions," *Harvard Business Review,* vol. 45, Dec.

Yin, R. K. (1981) "The Case Study as a Serious Research Strategy," *Knowledge: Creation, Diffusion, Utilization,* vol. 3, no. 1.

Zajonc, R. B. (1980) "Feeling and Thinking," *American Psychologist*, Feb.

Zajonc, R. B. (1984) "On the Primacy of Affect," *American Psychologist*, Feb.

Zaleznick, A. and M. F. R. Kets de Vries (1975) *Power and the Corporate Mind*, New York: Houghton Mifflin.

Zaleznik, A. (1989) *The Managerial Mystique*, New York: Harper and Row.

Zaleznik, A. (1977) "Managers and Leaders: Are They Different?" *Harvard Business Review*, May–June.

Zaleznik, A. and M. Kets de Vries (1984) "Leadership and Executive Action" in M. Kets De Vries (ed.) *The Irrational Executive*. New York: International Universities Press.

Zaleznik, A. (1990) "The Leadership Gap," *Academy of Management Executive*, vol. 4, no. 1.

Index